Sourdough Cookery

by Rita Davenport

HPBooks

Contents

ANOTHER BEST-SELLING VOLUME FROM HPBooks
Food Stylist: Mable Hoffman; Photography: deGennaro Associates; Recipe testing and revision: Dr. Ann Tinsley, R.D.

HPBooks are published by
The Berkley Publishing Group, 200 Madison Avenue
New York, New York 10016
ISBN 0-89586-155-0
Library of Congress Card Catalog Number 81-84969
© 1981, 1977 Price Stern Sloan, Inc.

Printed by Dong-A Printing Co., Ltd, Seoul, Korea. Represented by Codra Enterprises

10 9 8 7 6 5

Cover Photo: Clockwise from center top: Basic Sourdough Starter, page 15; Dinner Rolls, page 60; Sweet & Spicy Raisin Braid, page 38; Orange Candy Cookies, page 124; Chocolate Balls, page 123; San Francisco-Style French Bread, page 23; Cherry Rose Rolls, page 72

Rita Davenport

Rita Davenport's life has been devoted to the study of success principles. As a seminar leader, keynote speaker, author and home economist, she is a nationally recognized expert in the principles of success, time management methods, creative thinking, and building self-esteem and confidence. Her careers range from social work and teaching, to broadcasting and writing. She produced and hosted her own award-winning television shows, "Cooking with Rita" and "Open House," in Phoenix, Arizona for 15 years, and was viewed in over 32 million homes on her cable television show "Success Strategies" and infomercial "Laugh Your Way to Success."

Rita has also written five best-selling books with sales over two million copies.

A graduate of Middle Tennessee State University, Rita has done graduate work at Florida and Arizona State universities. She has taught Home Economics at both the high school and college levels.

Rita's passion for cooking started when she was just a child. It is the one hobby that she still manages to find time for in her busy schedule. To Rita, cooking is an expression of love...it comes straight from the heart.

Rita lives in Scottsdale, Arizona with her husband and her two sons, Michael, 13, and Scott, 11.

The Story of Sourdough

For centuries, sourdough was a mystery. According to one historical account, sourdough was discovered in the days of the Egyptian Pharaohs, about 5,000 years ago. An Egyptian noticed that some flour he left in an uncovered container had become wet. Bubbles had formed in the mixture of flour and water. Not wanting to waste the flour, the Egyptian used it to make bread dough. The bread baked from this mysterious dough had a light texture and a tantalizing flavor.

Today we know that moisture, *wild airborne yeast* and possibly some *lactic acid bacteria* fell into the open container of flour, causing fermentation. Yeast is a plant that ferments certain kinds of sugars in flour and produces carbon dioxide. This expands the dough in baked products, making them light and porous.

During the settlement of the American frontier, fresh yeast spoiled easily. Sourdough starter was used so frequently that it did not spoil. And it could be replenished. Miners and trappers carried a pot or crock of sourdough starter with them wherever they went. Each sourdough starter was carefully protected because it was a dependable and never-ending source of hotcakes, biscuits and bread. Because all of their meals depended on sourdough starter, these pioneers were appropriately nicknamed *sourdoughs*. Some starters became famous for their exceptionally good flavor. These starters were shared with friends and passed down from one generation to another. Today, some sourdough owners claim their starters are direct descendants of one of those pioneer starters.

Sourdough Today

Although sourdough is a heritage from our past, it's an enjoyable part in our lifestyle today. Sourdough is natural. Homemade sourdough products contain few or no preservatives. They are an inexpensive source of vegetable protein, carbohydrates, important minerals and B vitamins.

Let sourdough baking complement dinner from your electric slow-cooker or oven. Sourdough starter in yeast breads, quick breads and desserts gives these foods an interesting flavor. Quick breads and desserts are prepared as rapidly using sourdough as they are without it. The starter conveniently leavens and flavors your homemade yeast bread while you do other things.

Sourdough baking can be a means of relaxation. It may even become your new hobby. There is no limit to the unique and interesting recipes you can create from sourdough—breads, desserts, snacks, pancakes, rolls and a multitude of other delights. Experiment, create and enjoy sourdough.

Cherry Rose Rolls, page 72.

Baking with Sourdough

The basic ingredients in many sourdough recipes are sourdough starter, flour, liquid, sugar, eggs, fat and salt. Use the best available ingredients. The finished product is only as good as the ingredients that go into it.

Sourdough Starter can be obtained by mixing the ingredients together yourself or by obtaining a cup of starter from someone else. The older the starter, the more tangy the flavor.

Because of variations in flour, water composition and local atmospheric conditions, you may find one starter recipe works better for you than another. Starter recipes begin on page 13.

Flour is the major ingredient in most sourdough recipes. All-purpose or whole-wheat flours are used in all recipes. Rye flour is used in combination with wheat flour in some breads. See page 20 for information on wheat flour and yeast breads.

Stir flour gently before measuring it to eliminate the need for sifting. Flour may be sifted with other dry ingredients, or all dry ingredients may be stirred together until evenly distributed.

Milk, water or fruit juices are used in most sourdough recipes. Potato cooking water or milk may be used in bread recipes in this book that call for water.

Sugar and other sweeteners provide flavor, color and texture in baked foods. Each sweetener has a delicate but distinctive flavor. Sugar blends well with the flavors of other ingredients. Honey and molasses are used as substitutes in several breads and cookies.

Butter, margarine, shortening or oil are used to tenderize baked products and to enhance the flavors of other ingredients.

Temperature is an important factor in the success of a sourdough recipe. Sourdough must ferment and rise at a temperature close to 85F (30C). A thermometer will be helpful in determining room temperature.

Mix sourdough recipes in glass, stoneware or plastic bowls using wooden or plastic spoons. Any prolonged contact with metal will change the flavor of sourdough.

Store sourdough starter in a stoneware, glass or plastic container. Traditionally, stoneware crocks have been used, but a covered plastic pitcher or other plastic container will work just as well. *Metal containers should never be used.* There is a reaction between metal and the acid in sourdough starter. The container should be large enough to allow for expansion of the starter to twice its original size. Be sure there is a small hole in the top of the container or the lid is ajar to let accumulated gas escape and for the yeast to get air. If other people use your refrigerator, label the container so your starter won't be thrown out accidentally.

Use glass or metal baking pans for baking sourdough foods. Radiant heat in ovens passes through glass more readily than through metal. Foods baked in glass pans brown rapidly and result in thick crusts unless the oven temperature is lowered 25F (5C) from the recommended temperature. Cakes should be baked in pans with straight sides to get level tops that are evenly browned.

When choosing bowls and pans for sourdough breads, keep in mind that the dough will double in size before baking. If dough is to be refrigerated, be sure the container is two to three times larger than the amount of dough. As with other breads, sourdough bread rises slightly in the oven.

Making Sourdough Yeast Breads

Homemade breads take time and patience, but are worth the effort. The aroma of freshly baked bread adds interest to a meal, but the tangy flavor of sourdough adds excitement.

Sourdough yeast breads are made like other yeast breads. However, if the sourdough is the only leavening used, it takes several hours for the bread to rise. Active dry yeast is included in the recipes in this book to shorten the rising time.

Follow the recommendations given here to make some of the best bread you have ever eaten.

Mixing and Kneading—Use an electric mixer to combine softened yeast, liquid, sourdough starter and some of the dry ingredients. Beat the mixture on medium speed, adding flour one-half to one cup at a time until the dough becomes stiff and begins to climb the beaters. This helps to develop the gluten and shortens kneading time.

Use a wooden spoon to stir in more flour until the dough is no longer sticky and pulls away from the side of the bowl.

Turn the dough out onto a lightly floured surface. With floured hands, fold the side of the dough farthest from you over the dough closest to you. Press down firmly on top of the dough with the palms and heels of your hands while gently pushing away from you. Turn the dough one-fourth turn. Again fold the side of the dough farthest from you over the dough closest to you. Press down while gently pushing away from you. Repeat turning, folding, pressing and pushing until the dough becomes smooth and small bubbles form under the surface of the dough. This will take five to ten minutes.

Rising—Shape the kneaded dough into a smooth ball. Place the ball in a warm bowl that has been greased. Turn the dough to coat the entire surface with grease. This will prevent the dough from becoming dry. Cover the bowl with a dry cloth towel.

Dough rises best at 80 to 85F (25 to 30C). If your kitchen is cool, place the dough on a rack over another bowl containing warm—not boiling—water. This can be done on a counter or in an oven. Change the water as it cools.

Do not expose rising dough to direct heat. If it rises too fast, the result may be poor texture, appearance and flavor. Do not expose the dough to drafts. Cool air will delay rising and may kill the yeast.

Proofing or Testing—When the dough has doubled in size, test it by pressing two fingers into the center of the dough. If the indentation remains when you remove your fingers, the dough is ready to proceed. If the dough springs back most of the way, let it rise another 15 to 20 minutes.

Punch Down—This means exactly what it says. Make a fist with your hand. Punch the dough down in the center of the bowl, then pull the dough from the side of the bowl to the center. Punch it down again. Air pockets left in dough cause large holes when the bread is baked. Turn the dough out onto a very lightly floured board. The less flour you use at this time, the fewer dry streaks your bread will have in it.

Shaping Dough—Divide the dough into as many pieces as the recipe calls for. Shape one

How to Make Sourdough Yeast Breads

1/Use an electric mixer to beat in flour until dough becomes stiff and begins to climb beaters.

2/Use a wooden spoon to stir in more flour until dough pulls away from side of the bowl.

3/To knead dough, fold it toward you, then push down and away with the heels of your hands. Turn dough 1/4 turn.

4/Continue folding, pushing and turning until dough is smooth and elastic. Shape into a ball before placing in bowl.

5/When dough has doubled in size, test it by pressing two fingers into the center of the dough.

6/If indentation remains, dough is ready to proceed. If dough springs back, let it rise 10 to 15 minutes longer.

7/Punch down dough by pushing your fist into center. Pull edges of dough over center. Don't leave any air pockets.

8/Shape 1 loaf by rolling out dough on a floured board. Or pat gently into a rectangle with your hands.

piece at a time. Pat or roll out the dough to a rectangle as wide as your bread pan is long and twice as long as your bread pan is wide. If you have a 9" x 5" loaf pan, pat or roll the dough to a 9" x 10" rectangle. If you have a 7-1/2" x 4" loaf pan, make the rectangle 7-1/2" x 8".

Fold the two short sides to the center without overlapping them. Pinch the edges together. The dough can also be rolled jelly-roll fashion, starting with a short side. Place the dough seam side up in the greased loaf pan, then turn the dough seam side down. This greases the top of the loaf and gives a tender crust.

Rising of Shaped Loaves — Cover the loaf pan and dough with a dry cloth and set in a warm place free from drafts. Let the dough rise until it has doubled in size or has risen slightly above the top of the pan. If it rises too high or not enough, the shape and texture of your bread will not be good. See the box on Causes of Inferior Bread, page 12.

Bake your sourdough bread according to the directions in each recipe.

Good luck on your adventures with *Sourdough Cookery.*

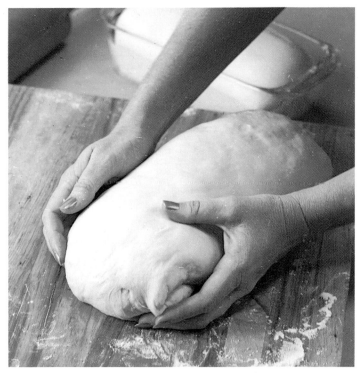

9/Fold or roll rectangle to fit loaf pan. Pinch edges together. Place seam side down in greased pan; grease top.

10/Place shaped loaves in a warm place free from drafts. Let rise until doubled in size.

11/Test by pressing edge of a loaf lightly with your finger. If dent stays, it has risen enough to bake.

Causes of Inferior Bread

Problem	Cause
Poor texture or color, low volume or heaviness	Inferior flour, oven temperature too low, over-rising, milk not scalded
Coarse texture or dry crumb	Too much flour, under-kneading, over-rising, milk not scalded
Undesirable flavor	Over-rising, inferior yeast or flour, too high temperature while rising, oven temperature too low, under-baked
Bread won't rise	Weak or inactive yeast, dissolving yeast in water that is too hot
Streaks through loaf	Poor mixing, under-kneading, too much flour on board, top of dough drying before shaping, using greased hands to shape loaves
Uneven shape	Too much dough for pan, improper molding or shaping, over-rising before baking, rising in a draft, pans touched in oven
Flat loaf that browns too quickly	Yeast killed with hot water, under-rising of loaf, over-rising of loaf which falls in center before completely baked
Porous bread with pale crumbling crust	Over-rising, too much flour, dough too stiff
Thick crust	Over-rising, under-kneading, oven temperature too low
Cracks in sides or top of crust	Dough too stiff, under-kneading, uneven heat in baking, too rapid cooling in draft
Tough crust	Inferior flour, too much salt, too much handling, needs more shortening
Pale crust	Too little sugar, too much salt, drying of dough during rising, oven heat too low
Bulging crust	Under-kneading, dough not punched down before shaping, loaf molded without removing gas bubbles, over-rising

Storing Sourdough Baked Goods

The absence of chemical preservatives and the presence of healthy, active yeast in sourdough call for special storage considerations. Here are three storing hints to keep your baked goods at their best:

- Sourdough products will keep for two or three days at room temperature in bread boxes or other containers that retard drying. Wrap baked goods securely in plastic wrap or foil.
- To keep baked items for several days, wrap them well and refrigerate them.
- Sourdough baked goods can be frozen up to three months.

Sourdough Starters

Sourdough starter is the beginning of all sourdough foods. It contains yeast plants and lactic acid bacteria similar to that which sours milk. Yeast needs a warm but not hot environment, moisture and a continuous food source. As yeast grows in the starter, it gives off carbon-dioxide gas, producing bubbles. This is what leavens sourdough bread.

In the wilderness, you can obtain these helpful yeast and bacteria by placing the basic flour and water mixture outdoors. Your only concern is that unfavorable bacteria may also invade the starter. If the mixture turns pink or orange, discard it immediately and start over. If you prefer to begin the starter indoors, add yeast to the flour and water mixture.

Many people prefer to mix up a fresh batch of Quick Overnight Starter each time they plan to do some baking. Others keep a container full of starter in their refrigerator available for use at a moment's notice. They use from the starter until about one cup remains, then replenish it. If you plan to keep it on hand, use and replenish the starter once a week and it will live indefinitely, gaining flavor and tang as it grows older.

To make a sourdough recipe, remove the amount of sourdough starter you need for the recipe. Refrigerate the remaining starter. If a clear liquid forms on top, simply stir it back into the mixture.

To replenish your starter, add equal amounts of flour and water to the container of sourdough starter. Stir with a wooden or plastic spoon. Cover the container with a cloth or plastic wrap. Puncture the plastic wrap two or three times to give the yeast air. Set overnight in a warm place free from drafts (85F, 30C). In the morning, stir down the mixture, cover it with a lid and return it to the refrigerator until it is needed. Do not add anything to the starter except flour and water and an occasional teaspoon of active dry yeast as needed to add life to the mixture.

If the starter is not replenished every seven to ten days, it may spoil. If this happens, discard the starter and begin with fresh ingredients. Don't discard the starter just because of its age. Merely replenish it.

Occasionally pour all of the sourdough starter into a mixing bowl. Wash the storage container to remove flour buildup. This is a good time to replenish the starter.

If you are not going to use the starter for a while, it can be stored in the freezer for up to three months. Before using, remove the starter from the freezer and let it thaw slowly in the refrigerator for 24 hours. Stir in equal amounts of flour and warm water. Let the mixture stand overnight in a warm place. In the morning, it will greet you with that familiar, appetizing sourdough aroma.

Basic Sourdough Starter   Photo on cover.

Use this starter in most of the recipes in this cookbook.

2 cups all-purpose flour
3 tablespoons sugar
1 envelope active dry yeast (1 tablespoon)

1/2 teaspoon salt, if desired
2 cups warm water (105F, 40C)

In a 4- or 6-cup plastic pitcher with a strainer in lid or in a large bowl, combine all ingredients. Beat with a wooden or plastic spoon. Fermentation will dissolve small lumps. Cover pitcher with lid, turning strainer in lid to pouring lip. Cover bowl with a cloth. Set in a warm place free from drafts (85F, 30C). Let ferment 2 to 3 days. Stir mixture several times each day. **To use,** remove starter needed for recipe. Refrigerate remaining starter in pitcher or in a plastic container with a lid that has an air vent or hole in it. Label container with contents. Replenish every 7 to 10 days by stirring in equal amounts of water and all-purpose flour. After replenishing, let stand at room temperature overnight. Return to refrigerator. If a clear liquid forms on top, stir back into starter. Makes 3 to 4 cups.

Quick Overnight Starter

Mild sourdough flavor in a hurry. Double the recipe if you plan to do lots of baking.

2 cups warm water (105F, 40C)
1 envelope active dry yeast (1 tablespoon)

2 cups all-purpose flour

In a 4- or 6-cup plastic pitcher with a strainer in lid or in a large bowl, combine all ingredients. Beat with a wooden or plastic spoon. Fermentation will dissolve small lumps. Cover pitcher with lid, turning strainer in lid to pouring lip. Cover bowl with a cloth. Set in a warm place free from drafts (85F, 30C). Let stand 6 hours or overnight. Starter will ferment, increase in size, then become thin and decrease to original size. **To use,** remove starter needed for recipe. Refrigerate remaining starter in pitcher or in a plastic container with a lid that has an air vent or hole in it. Label container with contents. Replenish every 7 to 10 days by stirring in equal amounts of water and all-purpose flour. After replenishing, let stand at room temperature overnight. Return to refrigerator. If a clear liquid forms on top, stir back into starter. Makes about 3-1/2 cups.

Variation
Use whole-wheat flour in place of all-purpose flour.

Starter at top is freshly mixed. As it ferments, bubbles form as shown at right. Fully developed starter is shown in center. When liquid forms on top, stir it back into the mixture.

Whole-Wheat Starter

Makes enough starter for any of the whole-wheat bread recipes.

1 cup warm water (105F, 40C)　　　　　　**1 cup whole-wheat flour**
1 teaspoon active dry yeast

In a 3- or 4-cup plastic pitcher with a strainer in lid or in a medium bowl, combine all ingredients. Beat with a wooden or plastic spoon. Fermentation will dissolve small lumps. Cover pitcher with lid, turning strainer in lid to pouring lip. Cover bowl with a cloth. Set in a warm place free from drafts (85F, 30C). Let stand 12 to 20 hours, stirring occasionally. **To use,** remove starter needed for recipe. Refrigerate remaining starter in pitcher or in a plastic container with a lid that has an air vent or hole in it. Label container with contents. Replenish every 7 to 10 days by stirring in equal amounts of water and whole-wheat flour. After replenishing, let stand at room temperature overnight. Return to refrigerator. If a clear liquid forms on top, stir back into starter. Makes about 1-1/2 cups.

Honey Starter

This is a popular starter with individuals who exclude sugar from their diets.

1 envelope active dry yeast (1 tablespoon)　　**2 tablespoons honey**
2-1/2 cups warm water (105F, 40C)　　　　　**2-1/2 cups all-purpose flour**

In a 2-quart plastic pitcher with strainer in lid or in a large bowl, combine all ingredients. Beat with a wooden or plastic spoon. Fermentation will dissolve small lumps. Cover pitcher with lid, turning strainer in lid to pouring lip. Cover bowl with a cloth. Set in a warm place free from drafts (85F, 30C). Let stand 1 to 2 days, stirring occasionally. **To use,** remove starter needed for recipe. Refrigerate remaining starter in pitcher or in a plastic container with a lid that has an air vent or hole in it. Label container with contents. Replenish every 7 to 10 days by stirring in equal amounts of water and all-purpose flour. Occasionally stir in 1 tablespoon honey. After replenishing, let stand at room temperature overnight. Return to refrigerator. If a clear liquid forms on top, stir back into starter. Makes about 3-1/2 cups.

How to Make Sourdough Starter

1/To begin your starter, mix dry ingredients in a bowl or pitcher. Stir in warm water.

2/Cover and let stand at 85F (30C) 2 to 3 days until mixture ferments and has a pleasant sour odor. Stir occasionally.

How To Replenish Sourdough Starter

1/Add equal amounts of flour and water to sourdough starter. Cover and let stand overnight.

2/In the morning, stir, then remove what is needed for recipe. Cover and store remaining starter in refrigerator.

Potato Water Starter

Use the potatoes for dinner and save the water for this starter.

3 medium potatoes, peeled, cubed
1 qt. water
1-3/4 cups all-purpose flour

1 tablespoon sugar
1 envelope active dry yeast (1 tablespoon)

In a large saucepan, cook potatoes in water until tender. Drain, reserving 2-1/2 cups liquid; set aside to cool. Use potatoes for another purpose. In a 2-quart plastic pitcher with a strainer in lid or in a large bowl, combine flour, sugar, yeast and reserved potato water. Beat with a wooden or plastic spoon. Fermentation will dissolve small lumps. Cover pitcher with lid, turning strainer in lid to pouring lip. Cover bowl with a cloth. Set in a warm place free from drafts (85F, 30C). Let stand 1 to 2 days or until mixture becomes bubbly. Stir mixture several times each day. **To use,** remove starter needed for recipe. Refrigerate remaining starter in pitcher or in a plastic container with a lid that has an air vent or hole in it. Label container with contents. Replenish every 7 to 10 days by stirring in equal amounts of water and all-purpose flour. Set in a warm place overnight. Return to refrigerator. If a clear liquid forms on top, stir back into starter. Makes about 3-1/2 cups.

Peasant Starter

Use this with recipes containing whole-wheat flour.

1 envelope active dry yeast (1 tablespoon)
1 tablespoon nonfat milk powder

1 cup whole-wheat flour
1-1/2 cups warm water (105F, 40C)

In a 2-quart plastic pitcher with a strainer in lid or in a large bowl, combine all ingredients. Beat with a wooden or plastic spoon. Fermentation will dissolve small lumps. Cover pitcher with lid, turning strainer in lid to pouring lip. Cover bowl with a cloth. Set in a warm place free from drafts (85F, 30C). Let stand 24 hours, stirring often. Mixture will be thick and bubbly. **To use,** remove starter needed for recipe. Refrigerate remaining starter in pitcher or in a plastic container with a lid that has an air vent or hole in it. Label container with contents. Replenish every 7 to 10 days by stirring in equal amounts of water and whole-wheat flour. After replenishing, let stand at room temperature overnight. Return to refrigerator. If a clear liquid forms on top, stir back into starter. Makes about 2 cups.

Rye Starter

Use with recipes containing rye flour for that true rye flavor.

1 cup rye flour   **1 teaspoon active dry yeast**
1 cup warm water (105F, 40C)

In a 1-quart plastic pitcher with strainer in lid or in a medium bowl, combine all ingredients. Beat with a wooden or plastic spoon. Fermentation will dissolve small lumps. Cover pitcher with lid, turning strainer in lid to pouring lip. Cover bowl with a cloth. Set in a warm place free from drafts (85F, 30C). Let stand 3 to 4 days or until mixture is frothy and has a pleasant sour aroma. **To use,** remove starter needed for recipe. Refrigerate remaining starter in pitcher or in a plastic container with a lid that has an air vent or hole in it. Label container with contents. Replenish every 7 to 10 days by stirring in equal amounts of water and rye flour. After replenishing, let stand at room temperature overnight. Return to refrigerator. If a clear liquid forms on top, stir back into starter. Makes about 1-1/4 cups.

tip
_____

If your starter is very tangy and you only want a mild sourdough flavor, add 1/2 teaspoon baking soda with the flour when you make yeast breads.

Yeast Breads

Sourdough starter used by itself works very slowly and the bread is sometimes quite firm and chewy. Adding yeast gives a lighter, more tender texture. Active dry yeast has been added to all of the yeast breads in this book. If you have a freshly fed and active starter and lots of time to let the bread rise without the added yeast, leave it out.

Although *active dry yeast* has been called for throughout the book, *compressed yeast* may be used in its place. Active dry yeast is more readily available than compressed yeast. It comes in small envelopes containing one tablespoon of yeast or in jars or cans. If kept tightly covered, active dry yeast can be stored in a cool dry place for up to one year. Compressed yeast comes in moist cake form and must be refrigerated.

Flour made from wheat contains a substance called *gluten*. When flour is mixed and kneaded with liquid, gluten forms an elastic framework that traps gas bubbles produced by yeast. This causes the bread to rise and achieves the desired light texture. Without gluten you cannot get a satisfactory yeast-raised or sourdough-raised bread.

Use water instead of milk in breads when you want a firm crust with good flavor. Rising time may be longer if hard, mineral-laden water is used. Soft water may make dough sticky or soggy. Potato water nourishes the yeast and promotes faster rising, but the dough may be darker than dough made with plain water. Be sure to strain most of the potato residue out of the water. If too much residue remains, it will prevent the development of the gluten.

Milk increases the food value of bread. The crust is softer and browner than when water is used. Milk that has not been scalded produces bread with a coarse texture. To scald milk, heat it to about 160F (70C). At this temperature, the surface shimmers and small bubbles begin to form around the edge of the pan. Cool the milk before combining with sourdough mixtures, or the heat will kill the yeast. Freshly opened canned evaporated milk and nonfat milk powder freshly mixed with water do not require scalding.

Sugar is not essential in bread but it adds flavor, supplies food for the yeast and promotes browning of the crust. White sugar, brown sugar, honey or molasses may be used.

Sourdough Bread

Delicious old-fashioned sourdough bread. Set the starter the night before.

Overnight Starter, see below
1 cup milk
3 tablespoons butter or margarine
3 tablespoons sugar
2 teaspoons salt

1 envelope active dry yeast (1 tablespoon)
1/4 cup warm water (105F, 40C)
6 to 7 cups all-purpose flour
Vegetable oil for tops of loaves

Overnight Starter:
1 cup sourdough starter
2 cups warm water (105F, 40C)

2-1/2 cups all-purpose flour

Prepare starter the night before according to directions below. Next morning, pour milk into a small saucepan. Heat almost to a boil over medium heat. Do not boil. Stir in butter or margarine, sugar and salt. Set aside to cool 10 minutes. Sprinkle yeast over water. Set aside to soften 5 minutes. Stir softened yeast mixture and cooled milk mixture into starter mixture. Beat until blended. Beat in 3 cups flour until batter is smooth. Cover with a cloth and set in a warm place free from drafts. Let rise 30 to 40 minutes or until almost doubled in size. Stir down dough. Gradually stir in enough remaining flour to make a medium-stiff dough. Turn out onto a lightly floured surface. Knead dough 8 to 10 minutes or until smooth and elastic. Add more flour if necessary. Divide kneaded dough in half. Cover and let rest 10 minutes. Grease two 9'' x 5'' loaf pans. Shape dough into loaves and place in pans. Brush tops lightly with oil. Cover with a cloth and set in a warm place free from drafts. Let rise about 1 hour or until dough reaches tops of pans. Preheat oven to 375F (190C). Bake 45 to 50 minutes or until loaves sound hollow when tapped with your fingers. After 30 minutes, if loaves are golden brown, cover with a tent of foil to prevent further browning. Remove baked loaves from pans. Cool top side up on a rack. Makes 2 loaves.

Overnight Starter:
In a large bowl, combine sourdough starter, water and flour. Cover with a cloth and let stand in a warm place overnight.

tip

When dough is set to rise, put it in a bowl twice as large as the ball of dough.

French Bread

Cornmeal sprinkled on the baking sheet will make you think of English muffins.

1-1/2 cups warm water (105F, 40C)
1 envelope active dry yeast (1 tablespoon)
1 cup sourdough starter
2 tablespoons sugar
2 tablespoons butter or margarine, melted

2 teaspoons salt
5 to 6 cups all-purpose flour
1 teaspoon cornmeal
Water for tops of loaves

Warm a large bowl. Pour 1-1/2 cups warm water into warmed bowl. Sprinkle yeast over water. Set aside to soften 5 minutes. Blend in sourdough starter, sugar, butter or margarine, salt and 2 cups flour. Stir in enough remaining flour to make a medium-stiff dough. Turn out onto a lightly floured surface. Clean and grease bowl; set aside. Knead dough 8 to 10 minutes or until smooth. Place kneaded dough in greased bowl, turning to grease all sides. Cover with a cloth and set in a warm place free from drafts. Let rise 1 to 1-1/2 hours or until doubled in size. Grease a large baking sheet. Sprinkle with cornmeal; set aside. Punch down dough. Cover and let rest 10 minutes. Shape into two 10" x 3-1/2" loaves. Pull ends out to make them narrower than center of loaf. Or shape into 2 round loaves. Place on prepared baking sheet. Cover with a cloth and set in a warm place free from drafts. Let rise about 1 hour or until almost doubled in size. Preheat oven to 375F (190C). Pour water 1 inch deep into a 12" x 7-1/2" baking pan. Place in bottom of pre-heating oven. Use a pastry brush to brush tops of loaves with water. Use a razor blade or very sharp knife to cut diagonal slashes across tops of loaves. Bake in preheated oven 30 to 35 minutes or until loaves sound hollow when tapped with your fingers. Remove from baking sheet. Cool on a rack. Makes 2 loaves.

Variation
To decrease the sourdough flavor, stir 1/2 teaspoon baking soda into first cup of flour added to yeast mixture.

Sourdough Croutons

Serve with a fresh salad.

1/2 cup butter
1/2 cup bacon drippings, strained
3/4 teaspoon paprika
3/4 teaspoon garlic salt

3/4 teaspoon celery salt
3/4 teaspoon sweet basil
2 cups cubed day-old sourdough bread
Parmesan cheese, if desired

Preheat oven to 400F (205C). Melt butter and bacon drippings in a 13" x 9" baking dish in pre-heating oven 3 to 5 minutes. Sprinkle in paprika, garlic salt, celery salt and sweet basil. Stir to blend. Add cubed sourdough bread; toss lightly to coat with herb mixture. Bake in preheated oven 5 to 7 minutes. Toss occasionally until all fat and spices are absorbed and cubes are browned. Sprinkle baked cubes with Parmesan cheese, if desired. Cool to room temperature. Store in an airtight container.

Variation
Prepare in your microwave oven by melting butter and drippings on High, about 25 seconds. Proceed as directed above. Bake coated bread cubes on High 1 to 2 minutes.

San Francisco-Style French Bread   Photo on cover.

French bread at its best.

1-1/2 cups warm water (105F, 40C)
1 envelope active dry yeast (1 tablespoon)
1 cup sourdough starter
2 teaspoons sugar

2 teaspoons salt
5 to 6 cups all-purpose flour
Water for tops of loaves

Warm a large bowl. Pour 1-1/2 cups warm water into warmed bowl. Sprinkle yeast over water. Set aside to soften 5 minutes. Stir in sourdough starter, sugar and salt. Beat in 3 cups flour until blended. Cover with a cloth and set in a warm place free from drafts. Let rise 1-1/2 to 2 hours or until doubled in size. Lightly grease a large baking sheet; set aside. Stir down dough. Stir in enough remaining flour to make a medium-stiff dough. Turn out onto a lightly floured surface. Knead dough 8 and 10 minutes or until smooth and elastic. Add more flour if necessary. Shape kneaded dough into two 10" x 3-1/2" loaves. Pull out ends of each to make them narrower than center of loaf. Or shape into 2 round loaves. Place on prepared baking sheet. Cover with a cloth and set in a warm place free from drafts. Let rise 1 to 2 hours or until almost doubled in size. Preheat oven to 400F (205C). Pour water 1 inch deep into a 12" x 7-1/2" baking pan. Place in bottom of preheating oven. Use a pastry brush to brush tops of loaves with water. Use a razor blade or very sharp knife to cut diagonal slashes across tops of loaves. Bake in preheated oven 45 minutes or until crust is golden brown and loaves sound hollow when tapped with your fingers. After 30 minutes, if loaves are golden brown, cover with a tent of foil to prevent further browning. Remove from baking sheet. Cool on a rack. Makes 2 loaves.

Cottage Cheese Bread

Delightful blend of cheeses and dill.

2 cups warm water (105F, 40C)
2 envelopes active dry yeast (2 tablespoons)
1 cup sourdough starter
2 cups creamed cottage cheese
2 cups shredded sharp Cheddar cheese or
   Longhorn cheese (8 oz.)

1/2 teaspoon baking powder
2 tablespoons dill seeds
2 tablespoons vegetable oil
2 tablespoons sugar
2 to 3 teaspoons salt
6-1/2 to 7-1/2 cups all-purpose flour

Warm a large bowl. Pour water into warmed bowl. Sprinkle yeast over water. Set aside to soften 5 minutes. Stir in sourdough starter, cottage cheese, Cheddar cheese or Longhorn cheese, baking powder, dill seeds, oil, sugar and salt. Beat in 6 to 7 cups flour, 1/2 to 1 cup at a time to make a stiff dough. Beat well after each addition. Turn out onto a lightly floured surface. Clean and grease bowl; set aside. Knead dough 8 to 10 minutes, adding remaining flour if necessary. Place kneaded dough in greased bowl, turning to grease all sides. Cover with a cloth and set in a warm place free from drafts. Let rise about 2 hours or until doubled in size. Generously grease two 9" x 5" loaf pans; set aside. Punch down dough. Shape into 2 loaves and place in prepared pans. Cover with a cloth and set in a warm place free from drafts. Let rise about 2 hours or until doubled in size. Preheat oven to 375F (190C). Bake 40 minutes or until loaves sound hollow when tapped with your fingers. After 30 minutes, if loaves are golden brown, cover with a tent of foil to prevent further browning. Turn out of pans. Cool top side up on a rack. Makes 2 loaves.

Cheese Swirl

Rolled filled loaves separate slightly as they bake.

1 teaspoon active dry yeast
3 tablespoons warm water (105F, 40C)
2 cups sourdough starter
3 tablespoons sugar
1 teaspoon salt
3 tablespoons nonfat milk powder

2 tablespoons vegetable oil or
  shortening, melted
3 to 4 cups all-purpose flour
1 cup shredded Cheddar cheese (4 oz.)
1 to 2 tablespoons dry onion soup mix
1 teaspoon butter or margarine, melted

Grease a 9" x 5" loaf pan; set aside. In a small bowl, sprinkle yeast over warm water. Set aside to soften 5 minutes. In a large bowl, combine sourdough starter, softened yeast mixture, sugar, salt, milk powder and oil or shortening. Beat until blended. Stir in flour 1/2 to 1 cup at a time to make a medium-stiff dough. Turn out onto a lightly floured surface. Knead dough 8 to 10 minutes or until smooth and elastic. Roll out kneaded dough to a 12" x 8" rectangle. Sprinkle evenly with cheese, then with onion soup mix. Roll up jelly-roll fashion beginning with a narrow side. Pinch edges together to seal. Place seam side down in prepared pan. Cover with a cloth and set in a warm place free from drafts. Let rise until doubled in size. Preheat oven to 350F (175C). Bake 50 minutes or until loaf sounds hollow when tapped with your fingers. After 30 minutes, if loaf is golden brown, cover with a tent of foil to prevent further browning. Turn out of pan. Place top side up on a rack. Brush top with melted butter or margarine. Serve hot or cold. Makes 1 loaf.

Variation

Cook and crumble 4 or 5 bacon slices. Sprinkle over soup mix before rolling dough.

Cheese Bread

Shred the cheese just before adding it so it doesn't pack down.

1-1/4 cups milk
1 envelope active dry yeast (1 tablespoon)
1/4 cup warm water (105F, 40C)
1-1/2 cups sourdough starter
1/4 cup sugar
2 teaspoons salt

1 egg, slightly beaten
3 tablespoons butter or margarine, melted
2 cups shredded sharp Cheddar cheese (8 oz.)
1/4 teaspoon baking soda
4 to 5 cups all-purpose flour
1 teaspoon butter or margarine, melted

In a small saucepan, heat milk almost to a boil over medium heat. Do not boil. Set aside to cool 10 minutes. Sprinkle yeast over water. Set aside to soften 5 minutes. In a large bowl, combine sourdough starter, cooled milk, sugar and salt. Beat well. Stir in egg, butter or margarine and cheese. Stir in softened yeast mixture. Add baking soda to 1 cup flour. Stir into sourdough mixture. Add remaining flour 1/2 to 1 cup at a time to make a medium-stiff dough, stirring after each addition. Turn out onto a lightly floured surface. Knead dough 8 to 10 minutes or until smooth and elastic. Add more flour if needed. Generously grease two 9" x 5" loaf pans; set aside. Divide kneaded dough in half and shape into 2 loaves. Place loaves in prepared pans. Brush with melted butter or margarine. Cover with a cloth and set in a warm place free from drafts. Let rise about 2 hours or until doubled in size. Preheat oven to 375F (190C). Bake 40 to 50 minutes or until golden brown and loaves sound hollow when tapped with your fingers. Turn out of pans. Cool top side up on a rack. Makes 2 loaves.

Half & Half Bread

You'll enjoy this mild, nutty, wholesome flavor. Bake the dough in loaves or as rolls.

2/3 cup nonfat milk powder
2 cups warm water (105F, 40C)
1 envelope active dry yeast (1 tablespoon)
3 cups whole-wheat flour
3 to 4 cups all-purpose flour
3/4 cup sourdough starter

1/4 cup molasses
1 tablespoon salt
3 tablespoons butter or margarine,
softened
1 teaspoon baking soda

In a large bowl, combine milk powder and water. Stir in yeast. Set aside to soften 5 minutes. Stir until yeast dissolves. Stir in whole-wheat flour, 1 cup all-purpose flour and sourdough starter. Beat until thoroughly combined. Cover with a cloth and set in a warm place free from drafts. Let rise 1 to 2 hours or until doubled in size. Stir down dough. Stir in molasses, salt and butter or margarine; set aside. Add baking soda to 1 cup remaining all-purpose flour. Stir into whole-wheat mixture. Gradually stir in enough remaining all-purpose flour to form a medium-stiff dough. Turn out onto a lightly floured surface. Clean and grease bowl; set aside. Knead dough 8 to 10 minutes or until smooth and elastic. Place kneaded dough in greased bowl, turning to grease all sides. Cover with a cloth and set in a warm place free from drafts. Let rise 1 to 2 hours or until doubled in size. Generously grease two 9'' x 5'' loaf pans; set aside. Punch down dough. Shape into 2 loaves and place in prepared pans. Cover with a cloth and set in a warm place free from drafts. Let rise about 2 hours or until doubled in size. Preheat oven to 375F (190C). Bake 45 minutes or until loaves sound hollow when tapped with your fingers. After 30 minutes, if loaves are golden brown, cover with a tent of foil to prevent further browning. Turn out of pans. Cool top side up on a rack. Makes 2 loaves.

Variation

Use Whole-Wheat Sourdough Starter, page 16, to increase nutty whole-wheat flavor.

Quick Sourdough Bread

An easy bread for the beginnner.

1 teaspoon active dry yeast
3 tablespoons warm water (105F, 40C)
2 cups sourdough starter
3 tablespoons sugar
1-1/2 teaspoons salt

3 tablespoons nonfat milk powder
2 tablespoons shortening, melted,
or vegetable oil
3 to 4 cups all-purpose flour

Generously grease a 9'' x 5'' loaf pan; set aside. In a small bowl, sprinkle yeast over warm water. Set aside to soften 5 minutes. In a large bowl, combine sourdough starter, softened yeast mixture, sugar, salt, milk powder and shortening or oil. Beat until blended. Gradually stir in enough flour to make a medium-stiff dough. Turn out onto a lightly floured surface. Knead dough 8 to 10 minutes or until smooth and elastic. Add more flour if needed. Shape into a loaf and place in prepared pan. Cover with a cloth and set in a warm place free from drafts. Let rise 1 to 1-1/2 hours or until doubled in size. Preheat oven to 350F (175C). Bake 50 minutes or until loaf sounds hollow when tapped with your fingers. After 30 minutes, if loaf is golden brown, cover with a tent of foil to prevent further browning. Turn out of pan. Cool top side up on a rack. Makes 1 loaf.

Oatmeal Bread

For a light texture, allow plenty of time for loaves to rise before baking.

1 cup milk
1 envelope active dry yeast (1 tablespoon)
1/4 cup warm water (105F, 40C)
1-1/2 cups sourdough starter
1/4 cup packed brown sugar
1/2 cup molasses

1 to 2 teaspoons salt
3 tablespoons shortening, melted, or
   vegetable oil
2 cups rolled oats
3-1/2 to 4-1/2 cups all-purpose flour
1 teaspoon butter or margarine, melted

In a small saucepan, heat milk almost to a boil over medium heat. Do not boil. Set aside to cool 10 minutes. Sprinkle yeast over water. Set aside to soften 5 minutes. In a large bowl, combine sourdough starter, cooled milk, brown sugar, molasses, salt and shortening or oil. Stir in softened yeast mixture. Add rolled oats 1/2 cup at a time, mixing well after each addition. Stir in 3-1/4 cups flour. Dough will be soft. Turn out onto a lightly floured surface. Clean and grease bowl; set aside. Knead dough 8 to 10 minutes or until smooth and elastic. Add more flour if necessary. Place kneaded dough in greased bowl, turning to grease all sides. Cover with a cloth and set in a warm place free from drafts. Let rise 2 hours or until doubled in size. Generously grease two 9" x 5" loaf pans; set aside. Punch down dough. Divide in half and shape into 2 loaves. Place in prepared pans. Brush tops with melted butter or margarine. Cover with a cloth and set in a warm place free from drafts. Let rise 1-1/2 hours or until loaves reach tops of pans. Preheat oven to 375F (190C). Bake 40 to 50 minutes or until lightly browned and loaves sound hollow when tapped with your fingers. After 30 minutes, if loaves are golden brown, cover with a tent of foil to prevent further browning. Turn loaves out of pans. Cool top side up on a rack. Makes 2 loaves.

Potato-Bacon Bread

Plan to have leftover mashed potatoes, then make this delectable bread.

2 envelopes active dry yeast (2 tablespoons)
1/2 cup warm water (105F, 40C)
1 cup sourdough starter
2 cups water
2 tablespoons vegetable oil or margarine,
   melted
2 tablespoons sugar

2 tablespoons salt
3 bacon strips, fried crisp, crumbled
   (1/2 cup)
2 cups shredded sharp Cheddar cheese or
   Longhorn cheese (8 oz.)
2 cups mashed cooked potatoes
7-1/2 to 9 cups all-purpose flour

Sprinkle yeast over 1/2 cup warm water. Set aside to soften 5 minutes. In a large bowl, combine sourdough starter, 2 cups water, oil or margarine, sugar, salt, bacon, cheese and mashed potatoes. Stir in softened yeast mixture. Stir in flour 1/2 to 1 cup at a time to make a medium-stiff dough. Turn out onto a lightly floured surface. Clean and grease bowl; set aside. Knead dough 8 to 10 minutes or until smooth and elastic. Add flour as needed. Place kneaded dough in greased bowl, turning to grease all sides. Cover with a cloth and set in a warm place free from drafts. Let rise 1-1/2 to 2 hours or until doubled in size. Grease three 9" x 5" loaf pans; set aside. Punch down dough. Shape into 3 loaves and place in prepared pans. Cover with a cloth and set in a warm place free from drafts. Let rise about 2 hours or until doubled in size. Preheat oven to 375F (190C). Bake 40 minutes or until loaves sound hollow when tapped with your fingers. After 30 minutes, if loaves are golden brown, cover with a tent of foil to prevent further browning. Turn baked loaves out of pans. Cool top side up on a rack. Makes 3 loaves.

Herb Twist

Careful blending of Italian seasoning and Cheddar cheese makes this a special loaf.

1 envelope active dry yeast (1 tablespoon)	**1 egg, slightly beaten**
1/3 cup warm water (105F, 40C)	**1-1/2 teaspoons Italian seasoning**
1 cup sourdough starter	**1 cup shredded Cheddar cheese (4 oz.)**
1/2 cup creamy onion-flavored salad dressing	**1 teaspoon salt**
1 tablespoon sugar	**3 to 4 cups all-purpose flour**

Sprinkle yeast over water. Set aside to soften 5 minutes. In a large bowl, combine sourdough starter and salad dressing. Stir in softened yeast mixture, sugar, egg, Italian seasoning, cheese and salt until thoroughly combined. Stir in flour 1/2 cup at a time to make a medium-stiff dough. Turn out onto a lightly floured surface. Clean and grease bowl; set aside. Knead dough about 2 minutes or until smooth and elastic. Place kneaded dough in greased bowl, turning to grease all sides. Cover with a cloth and set in a warm place free from drafts. Let rise 45 to 60 minutes or until doubled in size. Generously grease a 9" x 5" loaf pan; set aside. Punch down dough and divide in half. Shape each half into a 10-inch rope. Twist ropes around each other; pinch together at each end. Place twisted loaf in prepared pan. Cover with a cloth and set in a warm place free from drafts. Let rise 50 to 60 minutes or until doubled in size. Preheat oven to 375F (190C). Bake 30 to 40 minutes or until golden brown. Remove from pan immediately. Cool top side up on a rack. Makes 1 loaf.

Variation

Whole-Wheat Herb Bread: Use sharp Cheddar cheese. Replace flour with 2 cups whole-wheat flour and 1 to 2 cups all-purpose flour. Shape into a loaf as directed above or into 12 rolls. Bake rolls 25 to 35 minutes.

Bran Bread

Delicious way to include bran in your diet.

1 envelope active dry yeast (1 tablespoon)	**3 tablespoons butter or margarine, melted**
3/4 cup warm water (105F, 40C)	**1-1/2 teaspoons salt**
1 cup sourdough starter	**1-1/2 cups whole-bran cereal**
1/4 cup molasses	**2 cups whole-wheat flour**
3/4 cup nonfat milk powder	**1 to 2 cups all-purpose flour**
1 egg, beaten	

Sprinkle yeast over water. Set aside to soften 5 minutes. In a large bowl, combine sourdough starter, molasses and softened yeast mixture. Stir in milk powder, egg, butter or margarine and salt. Stir in cereal and whole-wheat flour. Stir in enough all-purpose flour to make a medium-stiff dough. Turn out onto a lightly floured surface. Clean and grease bowl; set aside. Knead dough 8 to 10 minutes or until smooth and elastic. Place kneaded dough in greased bowl, turning to grease all sides. Cover with a cloth and set in a warm place free from drafts. Let rise 1 to 2 hours or until dough is doubled in size. Grease a 9" x 5" loaf pan; set aside. Punch down dough and shape into a loaf. Place in prepared pan. Cover with a cloth and set in a warm place free from drafts. Let rise 1 to 2 hours or until dough is 1/2 to 3/4 inch higher than pan. Preheat oven to 375F (190C). Bake 30 to 40 minutes or until golden brown and loaf sounds hollow when tapped with your fingers. Remove from pan immediately. Cool top side up on a rack. Makes 1 loaf.

How to Make Herb Twist

1/Divide dough into 2 pieces. Shape each piece into a roll 10-inches long.

2/Twist rolls around each other. Pinch end together. Place twisted loaf in prepared pan.

tip

Process large pieces of whole-bran cereal in the blender before using them in bread dough.

Onion Twist

Cheese, onion and sesame seeds make this bread impressive in appearance and flavor.

1/2 cup milk	1/4 cup sugar
1 envelope active dry yeast (1 tablespoon)	1-1/2 teaspoons salt
1/4 cup warm water (105F, 40C)	1 egg, beaten
1 cup sourdough starter	4 to 5 cups all-purpose flour
1/2 cup water	Onion Filling, see below
1/2 cup butter or margarine, melted	2 teaspoons butter or margarine, melted

Onion Filling:

1/3 cup dried minced onion	1 tablespoon sesame seeds
1/4 cup butter or margarine, melted	1/4 teaspoon garlic powder
1-1/2 tablespoons grated Parmesan cheese	1 teaspoon paprika

In a small saucepan, heat milk almost to a boil over medium heat. Do not boil. Set aside to cool 10 minutes. Sprinkle yeast over 1/4 cup warm water. Set aside to soften 5 minutes. In a large bowl, combine sourdough starter, 1/2 cup water, 1/2 cup butter or margarine, sugar, salt, egg, cooled milk mixture and softened yeast mixture. Add 2 cups flour. Beat with electric mixer on low speed until blended. Beat 2 minutes at medium speed. Stir in enough remaining flour to make a medium-stiff dough. Shape into a ball. Leave ball of dough in bowl. Cover with a cloth and set in a warm place free from drafts. Let rise about 1 hour or until doubled in size. Prepare Onion Filling; set aside. Grease a large baking sheet; set aside. Stir down dough. Turn out onto a well-floured surface. Lightly knead dough 2 to 3 minutes. Add more flour if necessary. Roll out kneaded dough to an 18" x 12" rectangle. Cut lengthwise into three 18" x 4" strips. Spread filling evenly over strips, leaving 1 long edge of each strip uncovered. Starting with covered long edges, roll up each strip jelly-roll fashion. Pinch edges and ends to seal. Place strips on prepared baking sheet. Keeping seams inside, braid strips beginning at center and braiding to ends. Lightly pinch ends together. Cover with a cloth and set in a warm place free from drafts. Let rise 1 to 2 hours or until doubled in size. Preheat oven to 350F (175C). Bake 30 minutes or until golden brown. Remove baked loaf from baking sheet and brush with melted butter or margarine. Serve hot or cold. Makes 1 large loaf.

Onion Filling:
In a small bowl, combine all ingredients.

tip
_____

If fresh milk is used in yeast breads, scald it by heating until the surface shimmers. Cool before combining with yeast.

Raisin Casserole Bread

For variety, replace cinnamon and nuts with other spices and fruits.

1/4 cup milk	1 teaspoon salt
1 envelope active dry yeast (1 tablespoon)	1 egg, beaten
1/4 cup warm water (105F, 40C)	1/2 cup chopped walnuts or pecans
1 cup sourdough starter	1 cup raisins
1/2 cup sugar	1-1/2 teaspoons ground cinnamon
1/4 cup butter or margarine, melted	2-1/4 cups all-purpose flour

In a small saucepan, heat milk almost to a boil over medium heat. Do not boil. Set aside to cool 5 minutes. Sprinkle yeast over warm water. Set aside to soften 5 minutes. In a large bowl, combine sourdough starter, cooled milk, softened yeast mixture, sugar, butter or margarine, salt, egg, nuts and raisins until blended. Set aside. Stir cinnamon into flour. Beat flour mixture into sourdough mixture 1/3 at a time. Cover with a cloth and set in a warm place free from drafts. Let rise about 1 hour or until doubled in size. Grease a 1-1/2-quart casserole dish. Stir down dough. Turn into prepared casserole dish. Cover with a cloth and set in a warm place free from drafts. Let rise about 1 hour or until doubled in size. Preheat oven to 350F (175C). Bake in preheated oven 40 to 45 minutes or until golden brown. After 30 minutes, if loaf is golden brown, cover with a tent of foil to prevent further browning. Turn out of dish. Serve warm. Makes 1 loaf.

Pizza Bread

Marvelous Italian flavor. This bread and a fresh salad make a complete meal.

1/2 cup milk	1/4 teaspoon garlic powder
1 teaspoon active dry yeast	1/4 teaspoon Italian seasoning
2 tablespoons warm water (105F, 40C)	1/2 teaspoon dried leaf oregano, crushed
1 cup sourdough starter	2 tablespoons grated Parmesan cheese
2 tablespoons sugar	1/4 cup finely chopped pepperoni
1 teaspoon salt	2 to 3 cups all-purpose flour
1 egg, beaten	1 teaspoon butter or margarine, melted
2 tablespoons butter or margarine, melted	

In a small saucepan, heat milk almost to a boil over medium heat. Do not boil. Set aside to cool 10 minutes. In a small bowl, sprinkle yeast over water. Set aside to soften 5 minutes. In a large bowl, combine sourdough starter, cooled milk and softened yeast mixture. Add sugar, salt, egg, 2 tablespoons butter or margarine, garlic powder, Italian seasoning, oregano, Parmesan cheese and pepperoni. Constantly scraping side of bowl, beat 3 minutes by hand. Stir in flour 1/2 cup at a time until dough begins to leave side of bowl. Cover with a cloth and set in a warm place free from drafts. Let rise about 1 hour or until doubled in size. Grease a 9'' x 5'' loaf pan. Stir down dough. Spread evenly in prepared pan. Brush top with melted butter or margarine. Cover with a cloth and set in a warm place. Let rise 1 to 2 hours or until doubled in size. Preheat oven to 375F (190C). Bake 30 minutes or until golden brown. Turn out of pan. Cool top side up on a rack. Serve hot or cold. Makes 1 loaf.

Taco Twist

Hearty and strong-flavored. Delicious toasted over an open fire.

Overnight Starter, see below
1 envelope active dry yeast (1 tablespoon)
1/4 cup warm water (105F, 40C)
Taco Filling, see below
1-1/2 teaspoons salt

1/4 cup vegetable oil
1 (1-1/4-oz.) pkg. sour cream sauce mix
2 to 3 cups all-purpose flour
1 egg
1 tablespoon water

Overnight Starter:
1 cup sourdough starter
1 cup warm water (105F, 40C)

1 cup all-purpose flour

Taco Filling:
1/4 cup butter or margarine, melted
1 tablespoon taco seasoning mix
1/4 cup dried minced onion

1 tablespoon grated Parmesan cheese
1 teaspoon paprika

Prepare Overnight Starter the night before according to directions below. Next day, grease a large baking sheet; set aside. Sprinkle yeast over 1/4 cup warm water. Set aside to soften 5 minutes. Prepare Taco Filling; set aside. Stir softened yeast mixture into overnight sourdough mixture. Stir in salt, oil and sour cream sauce mix. Stir in enough flour to form a soft dough. Turn out onto a lightly floured surface. Knead dough 8 to 10 minutes or until smooth and elastic. Roll out kneaded dough to a 16" x 12" rectangle. Cut lengthwise into three 16" x 4" strips. Spread filling on each strip, leaving 1 long edge of each strip uncovered. Starting with covered long edge, roll up each strip jelly-roll fashion. Pinch edges and ends to seal. Place strips parallel to each other on prepared baking sheet. Keeping seams inside, braid strips beginning at center and braiding to ends. Lightly pinch ends together. Cover with a cloth and set in a warm place free from drafts. Let rise 50 to 60 minutes or until doubled in size. In a small bowl, beat egg. Beat in 1 tablespoon water. Brush egg mixture over surface of loaf several times as dough rises. Preheat oven to 350F (175C). Bake loaf 40 to 45 minutes or until golden brown. After 30 minutes, if loaf is golden brown, cover with a tent of foil to prevent further browning. Remove from baking sheet. Serve warm or cold. Makes 1 large twist.

Overnight Starter:
In a large bowl, combine sourdough starter, warm water and flour. Cover and let stand overnight.

Taco Filling:
In a small bowl, combine all ingredients.

Applesauce-Wheat Bread

Unsweetened applesauce is available in most supermarkets.

1 cup sourdough starter	3 cups whole-wheat flour
1/4 cup vegetable oil	1/4 teaspoon baking soda
1/2 cup packed brown sugar	1 envelope active dry yeast (1 tablespoon)
1-1/2 cups unsweetened applesauce	1/4 cup warm water (105F, 40C)
1 tablespoon salt	3-1/2 to 4-1/2 cups all-purpose flour
1 cup hot water (190F, 90C)	1 teaspoon butter or margarine, melted

In a large bowl, combine sourdough starter, oil, brown sugar, applesauce, salt, 1 cup hot water, whole-wheat flour and baking soda. Beat until thoroughly combined. Let rest 10 minutes. Sprinkle yeast over 1/4 cup warm water. Set aside to soften 5 minutes. Stir softened yeast mixture into sourdough mixture. Gradually beat in enough all-purpose flour to make a medium-stiff dough. Turn out onto a lightly floured surface. Clean and grease bowl; set aside. Knead dough 8 to 10 minutes, adding more flour if necessary. Place kneaded dough in greased bowl, turning to grease all sides. Cover with a cloth and set in a warm place free from drafts. Let rise 1 to 2 hours or until doubled in size. Grease two 9" x 5" loaf pans; set aside. Punch down dough. Divide in half and shape into 2 loaves. Place in prepared pans. Cover with a cloth and set in a warm place free from drafts. Let rise until almost doubled in size. Preheat oven to 350F (175C). Bake 35 to 45 minutes or until lightly browned and loaves sound hollow when tapped with your fingers. After 30 minutes, if loaves are golden brown, cover with a tent of foil to prevent further browning. Turn out of pans. Place top side up on a rack. Brush tops with melted butter or margarine. Cool before cutting. Makes 2 loaves.

Tomato-Cheese Bread

Surprising flavor to use for afternoon tea sandwiches.

2 envelopes active dry yeast (2 tablespoons)	2 to 3 tablespoons vegetable oil or margarine, melted
1/4 cup warm water (105F, 40C)	2 tablespoons sugar
1 (28-oz.) can tomatoes, undrained	1 tablespoon salt
1 cup sourdough starter	7 to 8 cups all-purpose flour
3 cups shredded sharp Cheddar cheese or Longhorn cheese (12 oz.)	

Sprinkle yeast over warm water. Set aside to soften 5 minutes. In a large bowl, cut tomatoes into pieces or mash with a fork. Stir in sourdough starter, cheese, oil or margarine, sugar and salt. Stir in softened yeast mixture. Beat in flour 1/2 cup at a time to make a stiff dough. Turn out onto a lightly floured surface. Clean and grease bowl; set aside. Knead dough 8 to 10 minutes, adding more flour if necessary. Place kneaded dough in greased bowl, turning to grease all sides. Cover with a cloth and set in a warm place free from drafts. Let rise 1-1/2 to 2 hours or until doubled in size. Generously grease two 9" x 5" loaf pans; set aside. Punch down dough. Shape into 2 loaves and place in prepared pans. Cover with a cloth and set in a warm place free from drafts. Let rise about 2 hours or until doubled in size. Preheat oven to 375F (190C). Bake 40 minutes or until loaves sound hollow when tapped with your fingers. After 30 minutes, if loaves are golden brown, cover with a tent of foil to prevent further browning. Turn baked loaves out of pans. Cool top side up on a rack. Makes 2 loaves.

Pumpernickel Bread

Serve this dark brown German bread with slices of mild-flavored cheese.

1 envelope active dry yeast (1 tablespoon)
1/2 cup warm water (105F, 40C)
1 cup sourdough starter
1 teaspoon salt
1/4 cup molasses
2 tablespoons vegetable oil

1 tablespoon caraway seeds
1-1/2 cups rye flour
1 cup whole-wheat flour
1 to 2 cups all-purpose flour
Vegetable oil for tops of loaves

Sprinkle yeast over water. Set aside to soften 5 minutes. In a large bowl, combine sourdough starter, softened yeast mixture, salt, molasses, 2 tablespoons oil and caraway seeds. Beat in rye flour and whole-wheat flour until combined. Stir in enough all-purpose flour to make a medium-stiff dough. Turn out onto a lightly floured surface. Clean and grease bowl; set aside. Knead dough 8 to 10 minutes or until smooth and elastic, adding more flour if necessary. Place kneaded dough in greased bowl, turning to grease all sides. Cover with a cloth and set in a warm place free from drafts. Let rise 1 to 2 hours or until doubled in size. Grease a 9" x 5" loaf pan; set aside. Punch down dough. Shape into a loaf and place in prepared pan. Brush top of loaf with oil. Cover with a cloth and set in a warm place free from drafts. Let dough rise 1 to 2 hours or until 1/2 inch above rim of pan. Preheat oven to 350F (175C). Bake 50 to 60 minutes or until loaf sounds hollow when tapped with your fingers. After 30 minutes, if loaf is golden brown, cover with a tent of foil to prevent further browning. Turn out of pan. Cool top side up on a rack. Makes 1 loaf.

Onion Bread

Toast and sprinkle with shreds of Cheddar cheese, then float on hot French onion soup.

2 cups milk
2 envelopes active dry yeast (2 tablespoons)
1/4 cup warm water (105F to 40C)
1 cup sourdough starter
3 cups shredded sharp Cheddar cheese or
    Longhorn cheese (12 oz.)

2 tablespoons vegetable oil or margarine,
    melted
2 tablespoons sugar
1 (1-1/4-oz.) pkg. onion soup mix
6 to 7 cups all-purpose flour

In a medium saucepan, heat milk almost to a boil over medium heat. Do not boil. Set aside to cool 10 minutes. Sprinkle yeast over water. Set aside to soften 5 minutes. In a large bowl, combine sourdough starter, cooled milk, softened yeast mixture, cheese, oil or margarine, sugar and onion soup mix. Beat in flour 1/2 to 1 cup at a time to make a medium-stiff dough. Turn out onto a lightly floured surface. Clean and grease bowl; set aside. Knead dough 8 to 10 minutes, adding more flour if necessary. Place kneaded dough in greased bowl, turning to grease all sides. Cover with a cloth and set in a warm place free from drafts. Let rise 1 to 2 hours or until doubled in size. Generously grease two 9" x 5" loaf pans; set aside. Punch down dough. Shape into 2 loaves. Place in prepared pans. Cover and let rise about 2 hours or until doubled in size. Preheat oven to 375F (190C). Bake 40 to 50 minutes or until loaves sound hollow when tapped with your fingers. After 30 minutes, if loaves are golden brown, cover with a tent of foil to prevent further browning. Turn out of pans. Cool top side up on a rack. Makes 2 loaves.

Oatmeal & Whole-Wheat Bread

Nutritious and delicious. Serve it toasted for breakfast.

1-1/4 cups boiling water
1 cup rolled oats
2/3 cup molasses
1/3 cup vegetable oil
2 teaspoons salt
2 envelopes active dry yeast (2 tablespoons)
1/2 cup warm water (105F, 40C)

1 cup sourdough starter
2 eggs, beaten
3 cups whole-wheat flour
2-1/2 to 3-1/2 cups all-purpose flour
6 tablespoons rolled oats
1 egg white
1 tablespoon water

In a medium bowl, combine 1-1/4 cups boiling water, 1 cup rolled oats, molasses, oil and salt. Set aside to cool 15 to 20 minutes. Sprinkle yeast over 1/2 cup warm water. Set aside to soften 5 minutes. In a large bowl, combine sourdough starter, cooled oats mixture and softened yeast mixture. Add eggs; beat well. Stir in whole-wheat flour. Stir in enough all-purpose flour to make a soft dough. Turn out onto a lightly floured surface. Clean and lightly grease bowl; set aside. Knead dough 8 to 10 minutes or until smooth and elastic. Add more all-purpose flour if needed. Place kneaded dough in greased bowl, turning to grease all sides. Cover with a cloth and set in a warm place free from drafts. Let rise 1 to 2 hours or until doubled in size. Punch down dough. Turn out onto a lightly floured surface. Cover and let rest 10 minutes. Generously grease two 9" x 5" loaf pans. Coat each prepared pan with 2 tablespoons rolled oats; set aside. Shape dough into 2 loaves. Place loaves in prepared pans. Cover with a cloth and set in a warm place free from drafts. Let rise about 1-1/2 hours or until doubled in size. Preheat oven to 375F (190C). In a small bowl, beat egg white. Stir in 1 tablespoon water. Brush tops of loaves with egg white mixture. Sprinkle 1 tablespoon rolled oats evenly over top of each loaf. Bake in preheated oven 40 to 50 minutes or until loaves sound hollow when tapped with your fingers. After 30 minutes, if loaves are golden brown, cover with a tent of foil to prevent further browning. Turn out of pans. Cool top side up on a rack. Makes 2 loaves.

tip

Milk scorches easily at high temperatures. Be sure to scald milk for breads over a low heat. Don't let it boil.

Onion-Rye Bread

Heavy and chewy with a tantalizing flavor. Use Rye Starter, page 19.

3/4 cup milk
1 envelope active dry yeast (1 tablespoon)
1/4 cup warm water (105F, 40C)
1 cup sourdough starter
2 tablespoons molasses
1-1/2 teaspoons salt

1/4 cup vegetable oil
2 tablespoons caraway seeds
3 tablespoons dried minced onion
1-1/2 cups whole-wheat flour
2 to 3 cups rye flour
Vegetable oil for tops of loaves

In a small saucepan, heat milk almost to a boil over medium heat. Do not boil. Set aside to cool 10 minutes. Sprinkle yeast over water. Set aside to soften 5 minutes. In a large bowl, combine sourdough starter, cooled milk, softened yeast mixture, molasses, salt, oil, caraway seeds, onion and whole-wheat flour. Stir in rye flour 1/2 cup at a time to make a medium-stiff dough. Turn out onto a lightly floured surface. Clean and grease bowl; set aside. Knead dough 8 to 10 minutes or until smooth and elastic. Place kneaded dough in greased bowl, turning to grease all sides. Cover with a cloth and set in a warm place free from drafts. Let rise 1 to 2 hours or until doubled in size. Generously grease a 9" x 5" loaf pan; set aside. Punch down dough. Shape into a loaf and place in prepared pan. Brush top lightly with vegetable oil. Cover with a cloth and set in a warm place free from drafts. Let rise 1 to 2 hours or until top is 1/2 to 3/4 inch above top of pan. Preheat oven to 350F (175C). Bake 45 to 50 minutes or until loaf sounds hollow when tapped with your fingers. In 30 minutes, if loaf is golden brown, cover with a tent of foil to prevent further browning. Turn out of pan. Cool top side up on a rack. Makes 1 loaf.

Variation

Use 2-1/2 cups whole-wheat flour and 1 to 1-1/2 cups rye flour.

Rye Bread

Equally good served warm or cold.

1-1/2 cups warm water (105F, 40C)
1 cnvelope active dry yeast (1 tablespoon)
1 cup sourdough starter
3 tablespoons sugar
3 tablespoons butter or margarine, softened

2 teaspoons caraway seeds
2 teaspoons salt
3 cups rye flour
2 to 3 cups all-purpose flour

Warm a large bowl. Pour water into warmed bowl. Sprinkle yeast over water. Set aside to soften 5 minutes. Stir in sourdough starter, sugar, butter or margarine, caraway seeds, salt and rye flour. Beat until blended. Add enough all-purpose flour to make a medium-stiff dough. Turn out onto a lightly floured surface. Clean and grease bowl; set aside. Knead dough 8 to 10 minutes or until smooth. Add more flour if necessary. Shape dough into a ball. Place in greased bowl, turning to grease all sides. Cover with a cloth and set in a warm place free from drafts. Let rise about 1-1/2 hours or until doubled in size. Grease two 9" x 5" loaf pans; set aside. Punch down dough. Turn out onto a lightly floured surface. Cover with a cloth and let stand 10 minutes. Shape into 2 loaves. Place in prepared pans. Cover with a cloth and set in a warm place free from drafts. Let rise 1 to 2 hours or until almost doubled in size. Preheat oven to 375F (190C). Bake 35 to 40 minutes or until golden brown and loaves sound hollow when tapped with your fingers. Remove from pans. Cool top side up on a rack. Makes 2 loaves.

Sweet & Spicy Raisin Braid   Photo on cover.

Perfect for a special brunch or breakfast.

1/2 cup milk
1 envelope active dry yeast (1 tablespoon)
2 tablespoons warm water (105F, 40C)
2 cups sourdough starter
1/4 cup packed brown sugar
1/4 cup butter or margarine, melted
1-1/2 teaspoons salt
1 egg, slightly beaten
1-1/2 cups raisins

1/2 cup chopped walnuts or pecans,
  if desired
2 teaspoons ground cinnamon
1/2 teaspoon ground nutmeg
4 to 5 cups all-purpose flour
1 tablespoon butter or margarine, melted
1 egg white, beaten
1 tablespoon granulated sugar

In a small saucepan, heat milk almost to a boil over medium heat. Do not boil. Set aside to cool 10 minutes. In a small bowl, sprinkle yeast over warm water. Set aside to soften 5 minutes. In a large bowl, combine sourdough starter, cooled milk, softened yeast mixture, brown sugar, 1/4 cup butter or margarine, salt, egg, raisins and nuts, if desired; set aside. In a small bowl, stir cinnamon and nutmeg into 1 cup flour. Beat into sourdough mixture until blended. Stir in enough remaining flour to make a medium-stiff dough. Turn out onto a lightly floured surface. Clean and grease bowl; set aside. Knead dough 8 to 10 minutes or until smooth and elastic, adding more flour if necessary. Place kneaded dough in greased bowl, turning to grease all sides. Cover with a cloth and set in a warm place free from drafts. Let rise about 2 hours or until doubled in size. Grease a large baking sheet; set aside. Punch down dough. Cut off 1/3 of dough; set aside. Divide remaining dough into 3 equal pieces. Roll each piece between your hands to make a 12-inch rope. Arrange ropes side-by-side on prepared baking sheet. Braid ropes beginning at center and braiding to ends. Lightly pinch ends together. Make a slight indentation through lengthwise center of braid by pressing lightly with the side of your hand. Set aside. Divide reserved dough into 3 equal pieces. Roll each piece between your hands to make three 7- to 10-inch ropes. Braid ropes together; pinch ends to seal. Carefully lift to top of larger braid, centering lengthwise. Brush all surfaces with melted butter or margarine. Let rise about 1 hour or until almost doubled in size. Preheat oven to 350F (175C). Brush surface of raised loaf with beaten egg white; sprinkle evenly with sugar. Bake in preheated oven about 40 minutes or until golden brown and loaf sounds hollow when tapped with your fingers. After 30 minutes, if loaf is golden brown, cover with a tent of foil to prevent further browning. Remove from baking sheet. Cool on a rack. Makes 1 large braid.

Variation

Grease two 9" x 5" loaf pans. Shape raised dough into 2 loaves. Brush surface of each loaf with melted butter or margarine. Follow remaining directions above. Makes 2 loaves.

Polish Sweet Bread

The flaired loaf resembles the skirt of a Polish peasant woman as she dances.

1/2 cup milk	2-1/2 cups all-purpose flour
1 teaspoon active dry yeast	3/4 cup sugar
1/4 cup warm water (105F, 40C)	1/2 teaspoon salt
1 cup sourdough starter	1/4 teaspoon ground cardamom
1/2 teaspoon vanilla extract	3/4 cup raisins
2 eggs, beaten	Nutmeg Topping, see below
1/4 cup butter or margarine, melted	

Nutmeg Topping:

1/4 cup sugar	1/2 teaspoon ground nutmeg
1/3 cup all-purpose flour	2 tablespoons butter or margarine

In a small saucepan, heat milk almost to a boil over medium heat. Do not boil. Set aside to cool 10 minutes. Sprinkle yeast over water. Set aside to soften 5 minutes. In a large bowl, combine sourdough starter, cooled milk, softened yeast mixture, vanilla, eggs and butter or margarine; set aside. In a small bowl, combine flour, sugar, salt, cardamom and raisins. Stir flour mixture into sourdough mixture. Beat until blended. Cover with a cloth and set in a warm place free from drafts. Let rise about 1 hour or until doubled in size. Prepare Nutmeg Topping; set aside. Grease an 8-cup Bundt pan or a 9" x 5" loaf pan. Stir down batter and turn into prepared pan. Sprinkle Nutmeg Topping over batter. Cover with a cloth and set in a warm place free from drafts. Let rise about 1 hour or until just to top of pan. Preheat oven to 350F (175C). Bake 30 to 40 minutes or until a wooden pick inserted in center comes out clean. Invert onto a rack. Remove pan. Cool to room temperature. Makes 12 to 16 servings.

Nutmeg Topping:

In a small bowl, combine sugar, flour and nutmeg. Cut in butter or margarine with a pastry blender or tines of a fork until mixture resembles coarse crumbs.

tip

Yeast doughs are doubled in size when an indentation made with your finger remains in the dough.

Sally Lunn

Delicious with butter and marmalade.

1 cup milk	1-1/2 cups sourdough starter
1 envelope active dry yeast (1 tablespoon)	3 eggs, beaten
1/4 cup warm water (105F, 40C)	1 teaspoon salt
1/2 cup butter	4-1/2 cups all-purpose flour
1/3 cup sugar	

In a small saucepan, heat milk almost to a boil over medium heat. Do not boil. Set aside to cool 10 minutes. Sprinkle yeast over water. Set aside to soften 5 minutes. In a large bowl, cream butter and sugar until smooth. Stir in sourdough starter and softened yeast mixture until combined. Stir in cooled milk and eggs; set aside. Stir salt into flour. Add to sourdough mixture; beat until smooth. Cover with a cloth and set in a warm place free from drafts. Let rise 1 to 1-1/2 hours or until doubled in size. Generously grease two 8-inch square baking pans, or one 9" x 5" loaf pan and one 7-1/2" x 4" loaf pan. Stir down batter. Pour into prepared pans until each is half full. Cover lightly with waxed paper and set in a warm place free from drafts. Let rise 1 to 1-1/2 hours or until just to tops of pans. Preheat oven to 350F (175C). Bake 45 minutes or until golden brown and surface springs back when touched with your fingers. After 30 minutes, if loaves are golden brown, cover with a tent of foil to prevent further browning. Serve hot or cold. Cut in wedges or slices. Makes 2 loaves.

Sunflower Seed Bread

Lovers of whole-wheat bread will make this bread often.

3/4 cup milk	2 tablespoons vegetable oil
1 envelope active dry yeast (1 tablespoon)	1-1/2 teaspoons salt
1/4 cup warm water (105F, 40C)	2/3 cup hulled sunflower seeds
1 cup sourdough starter	4 to 5 cups whole-wheat flour
1/2 cup molasses	

In a small saucepan, heat milk almost to a boil over medium heat. Do not boil. Set aside to cool 10 minutes. Sprinkle yeast over water. Set aside to soften 5 minutes. In a large bowl, combine sourdough starter, cooled milk, softened yeast mixture, molasses, oil, salt and sunflower seeds. Stir in flour 1/2 to 1 cup at a time to make a medium-stiff dough. Turn out onto a lightly floured surface. Clean and lightly grease bowl; set aside. Knead dough 8 to 10 minutes or until smooth and elastic. Add more flour if necessary. Place kneaded dough in greased bowl, turning to grease all sides. Cover with a cloth and set in a warm place free from drafts. Let rise about 2 hours or until doubled in size. Grease a 9" x 5" loaf pan; set aside. Punch down dough. Shape into a loaf and place in prepared pan. Cover with a cloth and set in a warm place free from drafts. Let rise 1 to 2 hours or until doubled in size. Preheat oven to 375F (190C). Bake 45 minutes or until loaf sounds hollow when tapped with your fingers. After 30 minutes, if loaf is golden brown, cover with a tent of foil to prevent further browning. Remove from pan. Cool top side up on a rack. Makes 1 loaf.

Rocky Road Loaf

The same flavor treat, but beats cold ice cream on a winter's night.

1/2 cup milk	3 to 4 cups all-purpose flour
1 teaspoon active dry yeast	1/3 cup granulated sugar
1/4 cup warm water (105F, 40C)	1/3 cup packed brown sugar
1 cup sourdough starter	2 teaspoons ground cinnamon
1/4 cup granulated sugar	1/4 cup butter or margarine, softened
1 teaspoon salt	2/3 cup chopped walnuts or pecans
1 egg	2/3 cup semisweet chocolate pieces
3 tablespoons vegetable oil	1 cup miniature marshmallows

In a small saucepan, heat milk almost to a boil over medium heat. Do not boil. Set aside to cool 10 minutes. Sprinkle yeast over warm water. Set aside to soften 5 minutes. In a large bowl, combine sourdough starter, cooled milk, softened yeast mixture, 1/4 cup granulated sugar, salt, egg and oil. Stir in enough flour to make a medium-stiff dough. Turn out onto a lightly floured surface. Clean and grease bowl; set aside. Knead dough 8 to 10 minutes or until smooth and elastic. Place kneaded dough in greased bowl, turning to grease all sides. Cover with a cloth and set in a warm place free from drafts. Let rise 1 to 2 hours or until doubled in size. In a small bowl, combine 1/3 cup granulated sugar, brown sugar and cinnamon; set aside. Generously grease a 9" x 5" loaf pan; set aside. Punch down dough. Turn out onto a lightly floured surface. Roll out dough to a 14" x 10" rectangle. Spread with butter or margarine. Sprinkle evenly with cinnamon-sugar mixture. Sprinkle evenly with nuts, chocolate pieces and marshmallows. Beginning on 1 long side, roll up jelly-roll fashion. Pinch edge and ends to seal. With seam side up, fold ends to center of roll. Place in prepared pan, smooth side down, to grease surface. Turn loaf over, placing folded ends on bottom. Cover with a cloth and set in a warm place free from drafts. Let rise 1 to 2 hours or until almost doubled in size. Preheat oven to 375F (190C). Bake 40 to 50 minutes or until top is golden brown and loaf sounds hollow when tapped with your fingers. After 30 minutes, if loaf is golden brown, cover with a tent of foil to prevent further browning. Let cool in pan 5 minutes. Remove from pan and cool top side up on a rack. Serve warm or cold. Makes 1 loaf.

tip

Whole-Wheat Starter, page 16, can be used with any of the bread or roll recipes.

Spinach Bread

The superb filling makes this a complete meal. Prepare the starter the night before.

Overnight Starter, see below
1/2 cup milk
1-1/2 tablespoons butter or margarine
1-1/2 tablespoons sugar
1 teaspoon salt
1 envelope active dry yeast (1 tablespoon)

1/4 cup warm water (105F, 40C)
3 to 4 cups all-purpose flour
Spinach Filling, see below
1 egg, beaten
1 tablespoon water

Overnight Starter:
3/4 cup warm water (105F, 40C)
1 cup all-purpose flour

3/4 cup sourdough starter

Spinach Filling:
1 (10-oz.) pkg. frozen spinach
1 egg, beaten
2 tablespoons grated Parmesan cheese
1/2 cup shredded mozzarella cheese (2 oz.)

3/4 cup diced pepperoni sausage
Garlic salt to taste
Pepper to taste

Prepare starter the night before according to directions below. Next morning, pour milk into a small saucepan. Heat almost to a boil over medium heat. Do not boil. Stir in butter or margarine, sugar and salt. Set aside to cool 10 minutes. Sprinkle yeast over 1/4 cup warm water. Set aside to soften 5 minutes. Stir softened yeast into cooled milk mixture. Stir into starter mixture until combined. Beat in 2 cups flour until batter is smooth. Cover with a cloth and set in a warm place free from drafts. Let rise 30 to 40 minutes or until almost doubled in size. Stir down dough. Gradually beat in enough of remaining flour to make a medium-stiff dough. Turn out onto a lightly floured surface. Knead dough 8 to 10 minutes or until smooth and elastic, adding more flour if necessary. Cover kneaded dough with a cloth. Let stand 10 minutes. Prepare Spinach Filling; set aside. Grease a large baking sheet; set aside. Roll out dough to a 12" x 10" rectangle. Spread filling over dough, leaving 1 long edge uncovered. Starting from covered long edge, roll up jelly-roll fashion. Pinch edges to seal. Place seam side down on prepared baking sheet. Cover with a cloth and set in a warm place free from drafts. Let rise until doubled in size. Preheat oven to 375F (190C). Combine beaten egg and 1 tablespoon water. Brush over surface of raised loaf. Bake in preheated oven 25 minutes or until golden brown and loaf sounds hollow when tapped with your fingers. Turn out of pan onto a platter or board. Serve hot. Makes 1 loaf.

Overnight Starter:
In a large bowl, combine water, flour and sourdough starter. Cover with a cloth and set in a warm place free from drafts. Let sit overnight.

Spinach Filling:
Cook spinach according to package directions. Drain cooked spinach in a fine sieve, pressing with back of a spoon to remove all water. In a medium bowl, combine well-drained spinach with remaining filling ingredients.

Quick Breads

Bread not leavened with yeast is a quick bread. This includes biscuits, muffins, griddle cakes, waffles and loaves. These breads contain baking powder or baking soda, both of which produce carbon dioxide gas when they become wet and hot. This gas causes the product to rise and become light and tender.

Flour mixtures are stirred into quick breads only until the dry ingredients are moistened. Overmixing batters that contain small amounts of liquid makes them tough and results in tunnels or holes in muffins and other quick breads.

A crack down the center of a nut bread or fruit bread is characteristic of quick breads. The crack can be made smaller by lining the greased loaf pan with waxed paper. Let the paper extend two to three inches above the pan on both sides. Grease the paper before pouring in the batter. As the bread bakes, heat is deflected from the top of the loaf by the waxed paper. This lets the dough rise in the center before the crust becomes firm.

These breads will slice easier if they are thoroughly cooled. Wrap the cooled loaves in foil or plastic wrap and let them sit several hours. This allows the flavors to blend and mellow.

If you prefer bread served hot with butter or a spread, warm the bread in an oven at 300 to 350F (150 to 175C) for about 5 minutes. Most fruit breads and nut breads are delicious toasted.

Unless a quick bread contains chocolate pieces or a soft fruit or vegetable, you can easily tell when it is done. Insert a wooden pick in the center of the bread. If it comes out free of dough, the bread is done. If the wooden pick is likely to pierce a soft ingredient, press gently on the center top of the bread. It will feel firm when it is done. When they are fully baked, some quick breads pull away from the side of the pan. Always check the crack along the center of the loaf. If you see uncooked dough in this crack, bake the loaf another 10 to 15 minutes.

Oatmeal-Apple Loaf

Also makes an excellent cake when you bake the batter in cake pans.

1 cup granulated sugar
1/2 cup shortening
2 eggs
1/2 cup sourdough starter
1 teaspoon vanilla extract
2/3 cup rolled oats
1 cup shredded or finely chopped
   unpeeled apple
1 cup all-purpose flour

1-1/2 teaspoons baking powder
3/4 teaspoon baking soda
1/2 teaspoon salt
1-1/2 teaspoons ground cinnamon
1/4 teaspoon ground nutmeg
3/4 cup chopped pecans or walnuts
2/3 cup powdered sugar
1 tablespoon milk

Generously grease a 9" x 5" loaf pan or a 9-inch square baking pan; set aside. Preheat oven to 350F (175C). In a large bowl, cream granulated sugar and shortening. Add eggs; beat until fluffy. Add sourdough starter and vanilla. Beat 1 minute with electric mixer on medium speed. Fold in rolled oats and apple; set aside. In a medium bowl, stir together flour, baking powder, baking soda, salt, cinnamon and nutmeg. Stir into sourdough mixture until just moistened. Fold in nuts. Pour into prepared pan. Bake in preheated oven 50 minutes for loaf pan or 35 to 45 minutes for square pan, or until a wooden pick inserted in center comes out clean. Turn out of pan. Cool on a rack 10 minutes. In a small bowl, blend powdered sugar and milk. Spread over loaf. Serve warm or cold. Makes 1 loaf.

Prune-Nut Bread

Slice and toast for a great way to start the day.

3/4 cup sugar
1/4 cup shortening
2 eggs
1/2 cup sourdough starter
1/4 cup fresh milk
1 cup all-purpose flour
1 teaspoon baking powder
3/4 teaspoon baking soda

1/2 teaspoon salt
1 teaspoon ground cinnamon
1/4 cup nonfat milk powder
1/2 cup wheat germ
1 cup cooked, drained, pitted prunes,
   chopped
1/2 cup chopped walnuts or pecans

Generously grease a 9" x 5" loaf pan; set aside. Preheat oven to 350F (175C). In a large bowl, cream sugar and shortening. Beat in eggs until thoroughly blended. Stir in sourdough starter and fresh milk; set aside. In a medium bowl, stir together flour, baking powder, baking soda, salt, cinnamon, milk powder and wheat germ. Stir into sourdough mixture until just blended. Fold in prunes and nuts. Pour into prepared pan. Bake in preheated oven 50 minutes or until a wooden pick inserted in center comes out clean. Turn out of pan. Cool top side up on a rack. Wrap cooled loaf in plastic wrap or foil. Let stand at room temperature 2 to 3 hours before cutting. Makes 1 loaf.

Lemon Loaf

Sweetened lemon topping emphasizes the lemon flavor and gives a moist texture.

1/2 cup shortening	1-1/3 cups all-purpose flour
1 cup sugar	3/4 teaspoon baking soda
2 eggs	1/2 teaspoon salt
1 cup sourdough starter	3/4 cup finely chopped walnuts or pecans
1/2 cup milk	Lemon Drizzle, see below
2 teaspoons grated lemon peel	

Lemon Drizzle:
1/4 cup sugar
1/3 cup lemon juice

Generously grease one 9" x 5" loaf pan or two 7-1/2" x 4" loaf pans; set aside. Preheat oven to 350F (175C). In a large bowl, cream together shortening and sugar. Beat in eggs until fluffy. Stir in sourdough starter, milk and lemon peel; set aside. In a medium bowl, stir together flour, baking soda and salt. Add to sourdough mixture. Beat 1 minute with electric mixer on medium speed. Fold in nuts. Turn into prepared pan or pans. Bake in preheated oven 1 hour or until a wooden pick inserted in center comes out clean. Prepare Lemon Drizzle. Puncture baked loaf 10 or 12 times with a sharp object. Pour Lemon Drizzle evenly over hot loaf. Let stand 5 minutes. Turn out of pan or pans. Cool top side up on a rack. Cool to room temperature before slicing. Makes 1 large or 2 medium loaves.

Lemon Drizzle:
In a small bowl, stir sugar into lemon juice until dissolved.

Granola-Prune Bread

Use Best-Ever Granola, page 157, in this delicious prune bread.

2-1/4 cups all-purpose flour	1/2 cup granulated sugar
3 teaspoons baking powder	1/4 cup packed dark brown sugar
1 teaspoon salt	1 cup sourdough starter
2 eggs	1-1/2 cups granola cereal
1 cup milk	1 cup chopped dried prunes,
1/4 cup vegetable oil	chopped dried apricots or raisins

Generously grease a 9" x 5" loaf pan; set aside. Preheat oven to 350F (175C). In a medium bowl, stir together flour, baking powder and salt; set aside. In a medium bowl, beat eggs. Stir in milk, oil, granulated sugar, brown sugar and sourdough starter. Stir in flour mixture. Beat 1 minute with electric mixer on high speed. Fold in granola and fruit. Turn into prepared pan. Bake in preheated oven 60 minutes or until a wooden pick inserted in center comes out clean. Turn out of pan. Cool top side up on a rack. Wrap in plastic wrap or foil. Let stand at room temperature 2 to 3 hours before slicing. Makes 1 loaf.

Mexican Corn Bread

Photo on page 57.

Colorful as well as tasty.

1 cup cornmeal
1 cup all-purpose flour
1 teaspoon baking powder
3/4 teaspoon baking soda
1 teaspoon salt
2 tablespoons sugar
2 eggs
1 cup sourdough starter

1-1/2 cups milk
1/4 cup vegetable oil
1 cup drained whole-kernel corn
1 medium onion, chopped
1 (4-oz.) can diced green chilies
1 (4-oz.) jar diced pimientos, drained
1-1/2 cups shredded Cheddar cheese (6 oz.)

Generously grease a 13" x 9" baking dish; set aside. Preheat oven to 400F (205C). In a medium bowl, stir together cornmeal, flour, baking powder, baking soda, salt and sugar; set aside. In a large bowl, beat eggs. Stir in sourdough starter, milk and oil. Stir in cornmeal mixture until just moistened. In medium bowl used for dry ingredients, combine corn, onion, chilies, pimientos and cheese. Fold into sourdough mixture. Pour into prepared baking dish. Bake in preheated oven 30 to 35 minutes or until surface springs back when touched with your fingers. Serve hot. Makes about 12 servings.

Corn Bread

This traditional Southern recipe should always be served piping hot.

3/4 cup yellow cornmeal
3/4 cup all-purpose flour
3/4 teaspoon baking soda
1/2 teaspoon salt
2 tablespoons sugar

2 eggs
1 cup sourdough starter
1 cup evaporated milk
1/4 cup butter or margarine, melted, or
    vegetable oil

Grease an 11" x 7-1/2" baking pan; set aside. Preheat oven to 450F (230C). In a large bowl, combine cornmeal, flour, baking soda, salt and sugar; set aside. In a medium bowl, beat eggs. Stir in sourdough starter, milk and butter, margarine or oil. Stir into dry ingredients until just blended. Pour into prepared pan. Bake in preheated oven 20 to 25 minutes or until a wooden pick inserted in center comes out clean. Serve hot. Makes 8 to 12 servings.

How to Make Mexican Corn Bread

1/Stir corn, onion, chilies, pimientos and cheese into sourdough mixture.

2/Pour mixture into prepared baking dish, being sure ingredients are distributed.

Hot Cheese-Onion Bread

Quick to prepare.

1 teaspoon active dry yeast	**4 cups biscuit mix**
1/3 cup warm water (105F, 40C)	**1/2 cup shredded Cheddar cheese (2 oz.)**
1 cup sourdough starter	**2 tablespoons sesame seeds**
1 (10-3/4-oz.) can condensed onion soup	

Grease a 9-inch square baking pan; set aside. Sprinkle yeast over warm water. Set aside to soften 5 minutes. In a large bowl, combine sourdough starter, condensed onion soup and softened yeast mixture. Stir in biscuit mix until just blended. Spread batter evenly in prepared pan. Sprinkle evenly with cheese, then with sesame seeds. Cover with a cloth and let rise 30 minutes. Preheat oven to 400F (205C). Bake 25 minutes or until a wooden pick inserted in center comes out clean. Serve hot. Makes 6 servings.

Corn Fritters

Use fresh corn for an old-fashioned fritter like Grandma made.

1 cup all-purpose flour
1/2 teaspoon baking soda
1/2 teaspoon salt
1/2 cup nonfat milk powder
2 eggs

1 cup sourdough starter
1 (12-oz.) can whole-kernel corn, drained
1/4 teaspoon dried minced onion
Vegetable oil for deep-frying

In a medium bowl, stir together flour, baking soda, salt and milk powder; set aside. In a large bowl, beat eggs. Stir in sourdough starter, corn and onion. Stir in flour mixture until just moistened; set aside. Pour oil 3 inches deep into a deep-fryer. Heat according to manufacturer's directions. Or pour oil 2 inches deep into a medium skillet. Heat to 375F (190C). At this temperature, a 1-inch cube of bread will turn golden brown in 40 seconds. Carefully drop batter by tablespoonfuls into hot oil. Fry 1-1/2 to 2 minutes on each side or until golden brown, turning once. Drain on paper towels. Serve hot. Makes 24 fritters.

Coconut-Carrot Loaf

For those who love coconut.

2 eggs
1/2 cup vegetable oil
1 teaspoon vanilla extract
1/2 cup milk
1/2 cup sourdough starter
2 cups finely shredded carrots
2 cups shredded coconut
1 cup raisins

1 cup chopped pecans or walnuts
2 cups all-purpose flour
1 teaspoon baking powder
1/2 teaspoon baking soda
1/2 teaspoon salt
1 cup sugar
1 teaspoon ground cinnamon
1/8 teaspoon ground nutmeg

Generously grease a 9" x 5" loaf pan; set aside. Preheat oven to 350F (175C). In a large bowl, beat eggs with electric mixer on medium speed until light in color. Add oil, vanilla, milk and sourdough starter. Beat until blended. Stir in carrots, coconut, raisins and nuts; set aside. In a medium bowl, combine remaining ingredients. Stir into sourdough mixture until dry ingredients are just moistened. Pour batter into prepared pan. Bake in preheated oven 1 hour or until a wooden pick inserted in center comes out clean. Turn out of pan. Cool top side up on a rack. Makes 1 loaf.

How to Make Corn Fritters

1/Heat oil to 375F (190C). Carefully drop batter by ta-blespoonfuls into hot oil.

2/Fry 1-1/2 to 2 minutes on each side or until golden brown. Turn once. Drain on paper towels.

Peanut Butter Bread

Two favorite flavors create this hearty treat.

1 cup boiling water
3/4 cup chunky-style peanut butter
3/4 cup nonfat milk powder
1 egg, beaten
1/2 cup sourdough starter
1/2 cup sugar

1-3/4 cups all-purpose flour
1 tablespoon baking powder
1 teaspoon baking soda
1/4 teaspoon salt
1 cup chopped salted peanuts

Generously grease a 9'' x 5'' loaf pan; set aside. Preheat oven to 350F (175C). In a large bowl, pour boiling water over peanut butter. Stir to blend. Stir in milk powder. Set aside to cool 15 minutes. Beat in egg, sourdough starter and sugar; set aside. In a medium bowl, stir together flour, baking powder, baking soda and salt. Stir into sourdough mixture until dry ingredients are just moistened. Fold in peanuts. Pour into prepared pan. Bake in preheated oven 40 to 50 minutes or until a wooden pick inserted in center comes out clean. Turn out of pan. Cool top side up on a rack. Wrap cooled loaf in plastic wrap or foil. Let stand at room temperature 3 to 4 hours before slicing. Makes 1 loaf.

Lettuce Loaf

This moist loaf is best if it stands several hours before it is sliced.

2-1/2 cups whole-wheat flour
2 teaspoons baking powder
1/2 teaspoon baking soda
1/2 teaspoon salt
1/8 teaspoon ground cinnamon
1/8 teaspoon ground ginger
1/8 teaspoon ground mace
2 eggs

1 cup sourdough starter
1 cup honey
1/2 cup vegetable oil
1 teaspoon grated lemon peel
1/2 cup milk
1 cup finely chopped lettuce
1/2 cup chopped walnuts or pecans

Grease and flour a 9" x 5" loaf pan; set aside. Preheat oven to 350F (175C). In a medium bowl, combine flour, baking powder, baking soda, salt, cinnamon, ginger and mace; set aside. In a large bowl, beat eggs. Stir in sourdough starter, honey, oil, lemon peel and milk. Stir in flour mixture 1/3 at a time, beating well after each addition. Fold in lettuce and nuts. Turn into prepared pan. Bake in preheated oven 50 to 60 minutes or until a wooden pick inserted in center comes out clean. Cool 15 minutes then turn out of pan. Cool top side up on a rack. Wrap cooled loaf in plastic wrap or foil. Let stand at room temperature 3 to 4 hours before slicing. Makes 1 loaf.

Zucchini-Nut Loaf

A tasty way to use vegetables. This bread stays moist for a week when it is kept wrapped.

1 egg
1/2 cup vegetable oil
1 cup sugar
1/2 cup sourdough starter
1 cup shredded unpeeled zucchini
1/2 teaspoon grated lemon peel
1/2 cup milk

2 cups all-purpose flour
1 teaspoon baking powder
1/2 teaspoon baking soda
1/2 teaspoon salt
1 teaspoon ground cinnamon
1/2 teaspoon ground nutmeg
1/2 cup chopped walnuts or pecans

Grease one 9" x 5" loaf pan or two 7-1/2" x 4" loaf pans; set aside. Preheat oven to 325F (165C). In a large bowl, beat egg slightly. Stir in oil, sugar, sourdough starter, zucchini, lemon peel and milk; set aside. In a medium bowl, stir together flour, baking powder, baking soda, salt, cinnamon and nutmeg. Stir into sourdough mixture until just blended. Fold in nuts. Pour into prepared pan. Bake in preheated oven 60 to 70 minutes or until a wooden pick inserted in center comes out clean. Turn out of pan or pans. Cool top side up on a rack. Wrap cooled loaf in plastic wrap or foil. Let stand at room temperature 3 to 4 hours before slicing. May be frozen or given as gifts. Thaw wrapped frozen loaves at room temperature 2 hours. Makes 1 large loaf or 2 medium loaves.

Variation

Carrot-Nut Loaf: Substitute 1 cup shredded carrots for zucchini.

Sopapillas

For a surprise treat, serve these puffed breads with a thick chocolate sauce.

1 cup all-purpose flour	**2 tablespoons shortening**
1-1/2 teaspoons baking powder	**1 cup sourdough starter**
3/4 teaspoon salt	**Vegetable oil for deep-frying**

In a large bowl, combine flour, baking powder and salt. Use a pastry blender or 2 table knives to cut in shortening until mixture resembles coarse crumbs. Stir in sourdough starter with a fork until dry ingredients are just moistened. Turn out onto a lightly floured surface. Knead dough 30 seconds or until smooth. Add more flour if necessary. Cover with a cloth and let dough stand 5 minutes. Pour oil 3 inches deep into a deep-fryer. Heat according to manufacturer's directions. Or pour oil 2 inches deep into a medium skillet. Heat to 390F (200C). At this temperature, a 1-inch cube of bread will turn golden brown in 20 seconds. As oil heats, roll out dough 1/4 inch thick. Or roll out to a circle with a 12-inch diameter. Cut into 3-inch squares or 4-inch wedges. Carefully lower 1 or 2 pieces at a time into hot oil. Fry 30 to 60 seconds on each side or until golden brown and puffed. Drain on paper towels. Makes about 20 sopapillas.

Serving Suggestion:
Serve with honey or sprinkle with powdered sugar or a mixture of 1/4 teaspoon cinnamon and 1/4 cup granulated sugar. When serving with honey, tear open one end or a corner of the sopapilla. Use a spoon or a honey dispenser with a long, thin spout to place some honey inside.

Hush Puppies

Serve with fish or other seafood.

1-1/2 cups cornmeal	**1 cup sourdough starter**
1/2 teaspoon baking soda	**1 egg, beaten**
1 teaspoon salt	**1/2 cup finely chopped onion**
1 teaspoon sugar	**Vegetable oil for deep-frying**
1/4 cup nonfat milk powder	

In a large bowl, combine cornmeal, baking soda, salt, sugar and milk powder. Stir in sourdough starter, egg and onion; set aside. Pour oil 3 inches deep into a deep-fryer. Heat according to manufacturer's directions. Or pour oil 2 inches deep into a medium skillet. Heat to 390F (200C). At this temperature, a 1-inch cube of bread will turn golden brown in 20 seconds. Carefully drop batter by tablespoonfuls into hot oil. If batter becomes too thick to drop from a spoon, stir in 1 to 2 tablespoons water. Fry hush puppies 1 to 2 minutes until crisp and golden brown. Turn to brown all sides. Drain on paper towels. Serve hot. Makes 6 servings.

Peach-Nut Bread

Delicious when spread with softened cream cheese.

1/2 cup boiling water
1 cup chopped dried peaches
1 egg
1 cup sourdough starter
1/2 cup packed brown sugar
1/2 cup granulated sugar
3 tablespoons vegetable oil
1/2 cup milk

2 cups all-purpose flour
1-1/2 teaspoons baking powder
1/4 teaspoon baking soda
1/2 teaspoon salt
1/2 teaspoon ground cinnamon
1/4 teaspoon ground nutmeg
1/4 teaspoon ground cloves
1 cup chopped walnuts or pecans

Grease and flour a 9'' x 5'' loaf pan; set aside. Preheat oven to 350F (175C). In a small bowl, pour boiling water over dried peaches. Soak 15 to 30 minutes or until plumped. Drain off excess water. In a large bowl, beat egg. Stir in sourdough starter, brown sugar, granulated sugar, oil, milk and soaked peaches; set aside. In a medium bowl, stir together flour, baking powder, baking soda, salt, cinnamon, nutmeg and cloves. Stir into sourdough mixture 1/3 at a time until just blended. Fold in nuts. Turn into prepared pan. Bake in preheated oven 40 to 50 minutes or until a wooden pick inserted in center comes out clean. Turn out of pan. Cool top side up on a rack. Wrap cooled loaf in plastic wrap or foil. Let loaf stand at room temperature 3 to 4 hours before slicing. Makes 1 loaf.

Poppy Seed Loaf

Lemon syrup adds a tart accent to this loaf.

3 eggs
1 cup sourdough starter
2 tablespoons poppy seeds
1 cup nonfat milk powder
1 teaspoon grated lemon peel
1/4 cup vegetable oil

5 tablespoons honey
1 teaspoon vanilla extract
1 teaspoon baking soda
1 cup all-purpose flour
Lemon Syrup, see below

Lemon Syrup:
1 cup sifted powdered sugar
2 tablespoons lemon juice

Generously grease a 9'' x 5'' loaf pan; set aside. Preheat oven to 350F (175C). In a large bowl, beat eggs. Stir in sourdough starter, poppy seeds, milk powder, lemon peel, oil, honey and vanilla; set aside. Stir baking soda into flour. Stir into sourdough mixture until just blended. Spread evenly in prepared pan. Bake in preheated oven 30 to 40 minutes or until a wooden pick inserted in center comes out clean. Prepare Lemon Syrup; set aside. Turn out of pan. Place loaf top side up on a rack. Pierce 10 to 12 times with a long thin probe. Drizzle warm syrup over top of warm loaf. Syrup will penetrate loaf and drip over sides. Makes 1 loaf.

Lemon Syrup:
In a small saucepan, stir powdered sugar and lemon juice over low heat until mixture comes almost to a boil.

Easy Pumpkin Loaves

Golden Glaze gives these loaves a beautiful topping.

1/2 cup granulated sugar
2 cups biscuit mix
1 teaspoon ground cinnamon
1/4 teaspoon ground allspice
1/4 teaspoon ground cloves
1 egg
1/2 cup sourdough starter

1/2 cup canned pumpkin
1/2 cup raisins
3/4 cup milk
2 tablespoons vegetable oil
1 cup chopped walnuts, if desired
Golden Glaze, see below

Golden Glaze:
2 cups powdered sugar
2 tablespoons half and half

3 to 4 drops yellow food coloring

Grease one 9" x 5" loaf pan, two 7-1/2" x 4" loaf pans or three 5-1/2" x 3" loaf pans; set aside. Preheat oven to 350F (175C). In a large bowl, combine sugar, biscuit mix, cinnamon, allspice and cloves; set aside. In a medium bowl, beat egg. Stir in sourdough starter, pumpkin, raisins, milk, oil and nuts, if desired. Stir into spice mixture until dry ingredients are just moistened. Turn into prepared pan or pans. Bake in preheated oven 35 to 40 minutes for small loaves or 50 to 55 minutes for other loaves. Bread is done when a wooden pick inserted in center comes out clean. Turn out of pan or pans. Cool top side up on a rack. Prepare Golden Glaze. Spread on cooled pumpkin loaf or loaves. Makes 1 large, 2 medium or 3 small loaves.

Golden Glaze:
Combine powdered sugar, half and half and food coloring. Only half of recipe is needed to glaze 1 large loaf.

California Bran Bread

Let this bread stand overnight and it will be easier to slice.

2 eggs
1/2 cup sourdough starter
1/3 cup vegetable oil
1/4 cup milk
1 cup mashed ripe bananas
1-1/4 cups all-purpose flour
1 teaspoon baking powder

1/2 teaspoon baking soda
1/2 teaspoon salt
2/3 cup sugar
1 cup whole-bran cereal, crushed
1/2 cup finely chopped dried apricots
1/2 cup chopped walnuts or pecans

Generously grease a 9" x 5" loaf pan; set aside. Preheat oven to 350F (175C). In a large bowl, beat eggs. Stir in sourdough starter, oil, milk and mashed bananas. In a medium bowl, stir together flour, baking powder, baking soda, salt and sugar. Stir into sourdough mixture until just moistened. Fold in cereal, apricots and nuts. Turn into prepared pan. Bake 1 hour or until a wooden pick inserted in center comes out clean. Turn out of pan. Cool top side up on a rack. Wrap in plastic wrap or foil. Let stand at room temperature 12 to 24 hours before slicing. Makes 1 loaf.

Banana-Nut Bread

Soda added to a recipe makes the sourdough flavor very mild.

1/3 cup shortening	1-1/2 cups all-purpose flour
1 cup sugar	1 teaspoon baking powder
2 eggs	1/2 teaspoon baking soda
1/2 cup sourdough starter	1/2 teaspoon salt
1 cup mashed bananas	1/2 cup chopped walnuts or pecans

Grease a 9'' x 5'' loaf pan; set aside. Preheat oven to 350F (175C). In a large bowl, cream shortening and sugar. Beat in eggs until blended. Stir in sourdough starter and bananas; set aside. In a medium bowl, stir together flour, baking powder, baking soda and salt. Stir into sourdough mixture until just blended. Fold in nuts. Pour batter into prepared pan. Bake in preheated oven 55 to 60 minutes or until a wooden pick inserted in center comes out clean. After 30 minutes, if top is golden brown, cover with a tent of foil. Turn out of pan. Cool top side up on a rack. Wrap in plastic wrap or foil. Let stand at room temperature 2 to 3 hours before cutting. Makes 1 loaf.

Variations

Whole-Wheat Banana-Nut Bread: Substitute 3/4 cup whole-wheat flour for 3/4 cup all-purpose flour.

Blueberry-Banana-Nut Bread: Fold in 3/4 cup blueberries with nuts. Thaw frozen blueberries before using; dry on paper towels.

Spicy Banana-Nut Bread: Stir 1 teaspoon ground cinnamon, 1/2 teaspoon ground allspice and 1/2 teaspoon ground nutmeg into flour mixture.

Orange-Banana-Nut Bread: Substitute 1/2 cup packed brown sugar for 1/2 cup granulated sugar. Add 1 tablespoon grated orange peel with sourdough starter and bananas.

Pumpkin-Mincemeat Bread

Delicious as a gift for the holidays. Include Ginger-Cheese Spread, page 70.

4 cups all-purpose flour	4 eggs
1 teaspoon baking powder	1/2 cup sourdough starter
1-1/2 teaspoons baking soda	2/3 cup water
1-1/2 teaspoons salt	1 cup vegetable oil
2 tablespoons pumpkin pie spice	2 cups canned pumpkin
1-1/2 cups granulated sugar	1-1/2 cups prepared mincemeat
1-1/2 cups packed brown sugar	1 cup chopped walnuts or pecans

Grease three 9'' x 5'' or five 7-1/2'' x 4'' loaf pans; set aside. Preheat oven to 350F (175C). In a large bowl, stir together flour, baking powder, baking soda, salt, pumpkin pie spice, granulated sugar and brown sugar; set aside. In a medium bowl, beat eggs. Stir in sourdough starter, water, oil and pumpkin. Pour all at once into flour mixture. Stir until dry ingredients are just moistened. Stir in mincemeat and nuts. Pour evenly into prepared pans. Bake in preheated oven 1 hour or until a wooden pick inserted in center comes out clean. Turn out of pans. Cool top side up on a rack. Wrap each cooled loaf in plastic wrap or foil as a gift or to freeze. Thaw wrapped frozen loaves at room temperature 2 hours. Makes 3 large loaves or 5 medium loaves.

Orange Drops

The delicious flavor of cake-like doughnuts without the bother of rolling and cutting dough.

1-2/3 cups all-purpose flour
2 teaspoons baking powder
1/2 teaspoon salt
1/3 cup sugar
1/4 teaspoon ground cinnamon
1/2 teaspoon ground nutmeg
1 egg

1/2 cup sourdough starter
1/2 cup milk
2 teaspoons grated orange peel
2 tablespoons vegetable oil
Vegetable oil for deep-frying
Honey Glaze, see below
1-1/2 cups shredded coconut

Honey Glaze:
1/2 cup honey
2 tablespoons boiling water

1-1/2 cups powdered sugar

In a large bowl, stir together flour, baking powder, salt, sugar, cinnamon and nutmeg; set aside. In a medium bowl, beat egg. Stir in sourdough starter, milk, orange peel and 2 tablespoons oil. Stir into flour mixture until blended. Pour oil for deep-frying 3 inches deep into a deep-fryer. Heat according to manufacturer's directions. Or pour oil 2 inches deep into a medium skillet. Heat to 360F (180C). At this temperature, a 1-inch cube of bread will turn golden brown in 60 seconds. Use 2 teaspoons to drop dough carefully by rounded teaspoonfuls into hot oil. If necessary, dip spoons into hot oil to keep dough from sticking. Cook dough until golden brown, turning with a fork as needed. Lift from hot oil with a slotted spoon. Drain on paper towels. Prepare Honey Glaze. Pour coconut into a pie plate. Dip cooked dough into warm glaze, turning to coat all sides. Roll each in shredded coconut. Cool on a rack. Makes about 36 drops.

Honey Glaze:
In a medium saucepan, heat honey over medium heat until thin. Add water and sugar. Cook and stir 3 to 5 minutes or until sugar dissolves.

Coffee Date-Nut Loaf

Delicious served with whipped butter or a mixture of honey and butter.

2 cups all-purpose flour
3 teaspoons baking powder
1/2 teaspoon baking soda
1 teaspoon salt
2/3 cup sugar
1/2 cup chopped walnuts or pecans

3/4 cup chopped pitted dates
1 egg
1/2 cup sourdough starter
1 cup cooled strong coffee
2 tablespoons shortening, melted, or
 vegetable oil

Grease a 9'' x 5'' loaf pan; set aside. Preheat oven to 350F (175C). In a large bowl, stir together flour, baking powder, baking soda, salt and sugar. Stir in nuts and dates. In a small bowl, beat egg. Stir in sourdough starter, coffee and shortening or oil. Stir into flour mixture until dry ingredients are just moistened. Turn into prepared pan. Bake in preheated oven 1 hour or until a wooden pick inserted in center comes out clean. Turn out of pan. Cool top side up on a rack. Makes 1 loaf.

Mexican Corn Bread, page 46.

Apricot Bread

Make ahead of time and freeze for unexpected guests.

1/4 cup boiling water
1/2 cup chopped dried apricots
1 egg
1/2 cup sourdough starter
1/2 cup milk
3 tablespoons vegetable oil
1/2 cup granulated sugar

1/2 cup packed brown sugar
1-1/2 cups all-purpose flour
1 teaspoon baking powder
1/4 teaspoon baking soda
1/4 teaspoon salt
1/2 cup chopped walnuts or pecans

Grease one 9" x 5" loaf pan, two 7-1/2" x 4" loaf pans or three 5-1/2" x 3" loaf pans; set aside. Preheat oven to 350F (175C). In a small bowl, pour boiling water over apricots. Set aside 30 minutes or until plumped. Drain off excess water. In a large bowl, beat egg. Stir in sourdough starter, milk and oil. Stir in granulated sugar and brown sugar; set aside. In a medium bowl, stir together flour, baking powder, baking soda and salt. Stir into sourdough mixture until just blended. Fold in plumped apricots and nuts. Turn into prepared pan or pans. Bake in preheated oven 40 to 50 minutes for small loaves or 50 to 60 minutes for other loaves. Loaves are done when a wooden pick inserted in center comes out clean. Turn out of pan or pans. Cool on a rack. Let baked loaves stand at room temperature 3 to 4 hours before slicing. Or wrap each cooled loaf in plastic wrap or foil as a gift or to freeze. Thaw wrapped frozen loaves at room temperature 2 hours. Makes 1 large, 2 medium or 3 small loaves.

Apricot-Oat Bread

Deliciously moist.

2-1/4 cups biscuit mix
1 teaspoon baking powder
3/4 cup sugar
1 cup rolled oats
1 egg

1/2 cup sourdough starter
1-1/4 cups milk
3/4 cup chopped dried apricots
3/4 cup chopped walnuts or pecans

Generously grease one 9" x 5" loaf pan, two 7-1/2" x 4" loaf pans or three 5-1/2" x 3" loaf pans; set aside. Preheat oven to 350F (175C). In a large bowl, combine biscuit mix, baking powder, sugar and rolled oats; set aside. In a medium bowl, beat egg. Stir in sourdough starter and milk. Stir into dry ingredients until just blended. Fold in apricots and nuts. Turn into prepared pan or pans. Bake in preheated oven 40 to 50 minutes for small loaves or 50 to 60 minutes for other loaves. Loaves are done when a wooden pick inserted in center comes out clean. Turn out of pan or pans. Cool top side up on a rack. Let freshly baked loaves stand at room temperature 3 to 4 hours before slicing. Or wrap each cooled loaf in plastic wrap or foil as a gift or to freeze. Thaw wrapped frozen loaves at room temperature 2 hours. Makes 1 large, 2 medium or 3 small loaves.

Rolls & Twists

Dough for rolls and twists is usually much softer and richer than bread dough. The gluten structure or framework of a loaf of bread must be strong to support its weight. Rolls and twists are small so the gluten does not have to be as strong.

For tender crusts, brush the tops of rolls or twists with melted butter or margarine before baking. For a crisp crust, brush with milk or with one egg beaten with one tablespoon of milk. A light coating of slightly beaten egg white before baking gives crust an appealing glow.

Some of the recipes give shaping suggestions. Others merely say to shape rolls. Follow the directions below for a variety of shaped rolls.

Pan Rolls—Roll out dough to a one-inch thick rectangle. Cut the dough into two-and-one-half-inch wide strips. Cut each strip into two-inch squares. Lightly flour your hands. Carefully stretch sides of the dough squares to the center bottom. Pinch the dough together on the bottom. Dip tops of the rolls in melted butter or margarine. Arrange them top side up in a greased baking pan with sides touching slightly.

Cloverleaf Rolls—Shape the dough into one-inch balls. Roll each ball in melted butter or margarine. Place three balls of dough in each greased muffin cup.

Fantans—Roll out dough to an eighth-inch thick rectangle. Generously brush with melted butter or margarine. Cut the dough into strips two inches wide. Stack four to six strips on top of each other. Cut the stacked strips into one-inch slices. Lay each stack of slices on its side in a greased muffin cup.

Parker House Rolls—Roll out dough one-half inch thick. Cut into two- to three-inch circles. Lay the thick edge of a table knife across the center of each circle. Press gently to make a groove, being careful not to cut through the dough. Brush each circle with melted butter or margarine. Fold the circles in half along the groove. Arrange the folded circles on a greased baking sheet.

Crescents—Roll the dough into a ten-inch circle one-fourth inch thick. Bush with melted butter or margarine. Cut into three-inch wedges. Roll up dough from the outside edge of each wedge. Arrange on a greased baking sheet with points of the wedges down.

Dinner Rolls Photo on cover.

Make these a part of your holiday dinner.

1 envelope active dry yeast (1 tablespoon)
1/2 cup warm water (105F, 40C)
1 egg
1 cup sourdough starter

2 tablespoons sugar
1 teaspoon salt
3 tablespoons butter or margarine, melted
3 to 4 cups all-purpose flour

Sprinkle yeast over water. Set aside to soften 5 minutes. In a large bowl, beat egg. Stir in sourdough starter, sugar, salt, butter or margarine and softened yeast mixture. Add 2 cups flour. Beat until smooth. Stir in enough remaining flour to make a soft dough. Turn out onto a lightly floured surface. Clean and grease bowl; set aside. Knead dough 5 to 8 minutes until smooth and elastic. Add more flour if necessary. Place in greased bowl, turning to grease all sides. Cover with a cloth and set in a warm place free from drafts. Let rise about 2 hours or until doubled in size. Grease a large baking sheet or two 9-inch, round baking pans; set aside. Punch down dough. Divide into 24 pieces. Shape each piece into a roll. Arrange on prepared baking sheet or in prepared baking pans. Cover with a cloth and set in a warm place free from drafts. Let rise 45 to 60 minutes or until doubled in size. Preheat oven to 400F (205C). Bake 20 minutes or until golden brown. Remove from baking sheet or pans. Serve warm. Makes 24 rolls.

Whole-Wheat Cloverleaf Rolls

Refrigerated dough takes about three hours to rise.

1-1/2 cups milk
1/2 cup butter or margarine
1/4 cup sugar
1-1/2 teaspoons salt
1 envelope active dry yeast (1 tablespoon)

1/4 cup warm water (105F, 40C)
3 eggs
1 cup sourdough starter
2-1/2 cups whole-wheat flour
3 to 4 cups all-purpose flour

In a small saucepan, heat milk almost to a boil over medium heat. Do not boil. Stir in butter or margarine, sugar and salt. Set aside to cool 10 to 15 minutes. Sprinkle yeast over water. Set aside to soften 5 minutes. In a large bowl, beat eggs. Stir in cooled milk mixture, softened yeast mixture, sourdough starter and whole-wheat flour. Beat until smooth. Stir in enough all-purpose flour to make a soft dough. Shape into a ball. Do not knead. Grease a 12- to 15-cup plastic container. Place dough in container, turning to grease all sides. Cover with a cloth and set in a warm place free from drafts. Let rise 1-1/2 to 2 hours or until doubled in size. Punch down dough. Cover with a tight-fitting lid or plastic wrap. Place in refrigerator overnight. Three hours before baking, grease 30 muffin cups; set aside. Pinch off dough to make 1-inch balls. Arrange 3 balls in each prepared muffin cup. Cover with a cloth and set in a warm place free from drafts. Let rise 2-1/2 to 3 hours or until doubled in size. Preheat oven to 400F (205C). Bake 12 to 15 minutes or until golden brown. Remove from muffin cups. Serve warm or cold. Makes about 30 rolls.

Variation

To bake without refrigerating: After rising first time, punch down dough. Shape into rolls as directed above. Cover with a cloth and set in a warm place free from drafts. Let rise 1-1/2 to 2 hours or until doubled in size. Bake as directed above.

Refrigerator Rolls

Bake this dough tomorrow or store it in the refrigerator and bake rolls all week.

2 envelopes active dry yeast (2 tablespoons)	**1 cup warm water (105F, 40C)**
1/2 cup warm water (105F, 40C)	**1/2 cup sugar**
3 eggs	**2 teaspoons salt**
1 cup sourdough starter	**4-3/4 to 6 cups all-purpose flour**
1/2 cup vegetable oil	**2 tablespoons butter or margarine, melted**

Sprinkle yeast over 1/2 cup warm water. Set aside to soften 5 minutes. In a large bowl, beat eggs. Stir in sourdough starter, oil, 1 cup warm water, sugar, salt and 2 cups all-purpose flour. Beat vigorously 1 minute. Stir in softened yeast mixture and enough flour to make a soft dough. Do not knead. Grease a 12- to 15-cup plastic container. Place dough in container, turning to grease all sides. Cover with a cloth and set in a warm place free from drafts. Let rise 1 to 1-1/2 hours or until doubled in size. Punch down dough. Cover with a tight-fitting lid or plastic wrap. Place in refrigerator overnight. Three hours before baking, grease 24 muffin cups; set aside. Punch down dough. Turn out onto a lightly floured surface. Divide dough in half. Roll out each half into a 12" x 6" rectangle. Spread evenly with melted butter or margarine. Starting with a long side, roll up each rectangle jelly-roll fashion. Cut into 1-inch slices. Place cut side down in prepared muffin cups. Cover with a cloth and set in a warm place free from drafts. Let rise 2-1/2 to 3 hours or until doubled in size. Preheat oven to 400F (205C). Bake 12 to 15 minutes or until golden brown. Remove from muffin cups. Serve warm or cold. Makes 18 to 24 rolls.

Herb Dinner Rolls

Delightfully different for a special dinner. Use half whole-wheat flour for a change.

1 envelope active dry yeast (1 tablespoon)	**2 tablespoons butter or margarine, melted**
1/4 cup warm water (105F, 40C)	**1/2 teaspoon celery seeds**
1 egg	**1/4 teaspoon dried leaf thyme, crushed**
1-1/2 cups sourdough starter	**1/2 teaspoon dried parsley, crushed**
1 tablespoon sugar	**3 to 4 cups all-purpose flour**
1/2 teaspoon salt	**1 tablespoon butter or margarine, melted**

Sprinkle yeast over water. Set aside to soften 5 minutes. In a large bowl, beat egg. Stir in sourdough starter, sugar, salt, 2 tablespoons melted butter or margarine and softened yeast mixture; set aside. Stir celery seeds, thyme and parsley into 1 cup flour. Stir into sourdough mixture. Stir in enough remaining flour to make a soft dough. Turn out onto a lightly floured surface. Clean and grease bowl; set aside. Knead dough 8 to 10 minutes or until smooth and satiny. Add more flour if necessary. Place in greased bowl, turning to grease all sides. Cover with a cloth and set in a warm place free from drafts. Let rise about 2 hours or until doubled in size. Grease a large baking sheet or a 13" x 9" baking pan; set aside. Punch down dough and shape into rolls. Arrange on prepared baking sheet or in baking pan. Brush with 1 tablespoon melted butter or margarine. Cover with a cloth and set in a warm place free from drafts. Let rise about 1-1/2 hours or until doubled in size. Preheat oven to 400F (205C). Bake 12 to 15 minutes until golden brown. Remove from baking sheet. Makes 18 to 24 rolls.

Cheese Taco Boats

You'll enjoy these flavorful foldovers.

1/2 cup milk
2 tablespoons butter or margarine
2 tablespoons sugar
1 teaspoon active dry yeast
2 tablespoons warm water (105F, 40C)
1 egg

3/4 cup sourdough starter
1/2 teaspoon salt
2 to 3 cups all-purpose flour
2 tablespoons butter or margarine, melted
Pepper-Onion Filling, see below
1 (1-1/4-oz.) pkg. taco seasoning mix

Pepper-Onion Filling:
1 (8-oz.) pkg. cream cheese
1/2 cup butter or margarine

2 tablespoons dried minced onion
1/4 cup chopped green peppers

In a small saucepan, heat milk almost to a boil over medium heat. Do not boil. Stir in 2 tablespoons butter or margarine and sugar. Set aside to cool 10 minutes. In a small bowl, sprinkle yeast over water. Set aside to soften 5 minutes. In a large bowl, beat egg. Stir in sourdough starter, salt, cooled milk mixture and softened yeast mixture. Stir in enough flour to make a stiff dough. Turn out onto a lightly floured surface. Knead 8 to 10 minutes or until smooth and elastic. Cover with a cloth and let stand 20 minutes. Prepare Pepper-Onion Filling; set aside. Pour taco seasoning mix into a small bowl. Stir to break up any lumps; set aside. Lightly grease two 13" x 9" baking pans; set aside. Punch down dough and shape into 1-inch balls. Roll out each ball to a 3-1/2-inch circle. Spoon 1 rounded teaspoonful filling onto 1 side of each circle. Fold other side of circle over filling, bringing edges together. Press edges with tines of a fork to seal. Brush tops with 2 tablespoons melted butter or margarine. Sprinkle with taco seasoning mix. Arrange buttered side up in prepared baking pans. Cover with plastic wrap, waxed paper or a cloth. Be sure cloth does not touch topping. Topping will stain cloth. Set in a warm place free from drafts. Let rise 50 to 60 minutes or until tops feel light and tender when touched with your fingers. Preheat oven to 375F (190C). Bake 18 to 20 minutes or until golden brown. Remove from pan. Cool on rack. Serve warm or cold. Makes 24 to 36 servings.

Pepper-Onion Filling:
Soften cream cheese. Stir in remaining ingredients.

Variation

After placing prepared boats in baking pans, refrigerate 2 to 24 hours. An hour before serving, let stand at room temperature 30 to 40 minutes. Bake as directed above.

tip

Unbleached flour can be used in place of all-purpose flour measure for measure.

How to Make Cheese Taco Boats

1/Roll out each ball of dough to a 3-1/2-inch circle. Spoon 1 rounded teaspoonful of filling onto 1 side of each circle.

2/Fold other side of circle over filling, bringing edges together. Press edges with tines of a fork to seal.

Old-Fashioned Sticky Buns

Just like Grandma used to make.

1 tablespoon butter or margarine, melted
1/3 to 1/2 cup packed brown sugar
1/4 cup chopped walnuts or pecans

7 to 9 walnut or pecan halves
12 unbaked Cinnamon-Nut Rolls,
   page 71 (1/2 recipe)

Pour butter or margarine into bottom of a 9-inch, round baking pan. Tilt pan to cover completely. Sprinkle brown sugar evenly over butter or margarine. Sprinkle evenly with 1/4 cup chopped nuts. Arrange walnut or pecan halves over bottom of pan. Arrange unbaked Cinnamon-Nut Rolls cut side down in pan, with sides touching. Cover with a cloth and set in a warm place free from drafts. Let rise about 1-1/2 hours or until doubled in size. Preheat oven to 400F (205C). Bake 25 to 30 minutes or until golden brown. Immediately turn out of pan onto a serving plate. Quickly spoon excess syrup over baked rolls. Makes 12 buns.

Hot Cross Buns

You can also add nuts and raisins to this traditional bread.

3/4 cup milk
1 teaspoon active dry yeast
1-1/2 cups sourdough starter
2 tablespoons sugar
1 tablespoon butter or margarine, melted
1 teaspoon vanilla extract
1 teaspoon salt
1/3 cup chopped red glacé cherries

2/3 cup currants
3-1/2 to 4-1/2 cups all-purpose flour
1 egg
2 tablespoons cold water
Powdered Sugar Glaze, see below
Red glacé cherries,
   cut in half for decoration
Currants for decoration

Powdered Sugar Glaze:
About 2 tablespoons milk
1-1/2 cups powdered sugar

In a small saucepan, heat milk almost to a boil over medium heat. Do not boil. Set aside until just warm, 10 minutes. Sprinkle yeast over warm milk. Set aside to soften 5 minutes. In a large bowl, combine sourdough starter, softened yeast mixture, sugar, butter or margarine, vanilla and salt. Stir in 1/3 cup chopped cherries and 2/3 cup currants. Stir in enough flour to make a soft dough. Turn out onto a lightly floured surface. Clean and grease bowl; set aside. Knead dough 5 to 8 minutes or until smooth and elastic. Add more flour if necessary. Place in greased bowl, turning to grease all sides. Cover with a cloth and set in a warm place free from drafts. Let rise about 2 hours or until doubled in size. Grease a large baking sheet; set aside. Punch down dough. Shape into 1-1/2-inch balls. Arrange about 3 inches apart on prepared baking sheet. Cover with a cloth and set in a warm place free from drafts. Let rise 1 to 1-1/2 hours or until doubled in size. In a small bowl, beat egg. Stir in water; set aside. Preheat oven to 400F (205C). Using a table knife, carefully press thin edge of blade across top of each raised bun, horizontally then vertically, making a cross. Do not cut dough or buns will collapse. Carefully brush buns with egg-water mixture. Bake in preheated oven 10 to 15 minutes or until golden brown. Prepare Powdered Sugar Glaze; set aside. Remove buns from baking sheet. Cool on a rack. Pour glaze into cross on each cooled bun. Decorate with halved cherries and currants. Makes about 18 buns.

Powdered Sugar Glaze:
In a small bowl, stir milk into powdered sugar 1 teaspoon at a time until mixture can be slowly poured from a spoon.

Variation
Arrange balls of dough in a 13'' x 9'' baking pan. Let rise as directed above. Do not score tops. Brush raised buns with egg-water mixture. Bake as directed above. Cool on a rack. Drizzle with glaze.

Bran Rolls

Makes a delicious dinner roll.

1 teaspoon active dry yeast	**3 tablespoons vegetable oil**
1/2 cup warm water (105F, 40C)	**1/2 cup whole-bran cereal**
1 egg	**1 teaspoon salt**
1 cup sourdough starter	**2 to 3 cups all-purpose flour**
2 tablespoons packed brown sugar	

Sprinkle yeast over water. Set aside to soften 5 minutes. In a large bowl, beat egg. Stir in sourdough starter, brown sugar, oil, bran cereal, salt and softened yeast mixture. Mix well. Stir in enough flour to make a soft dough. Turn out onto a lightly floured board. Clean and grease bowl; set aside. Knead dough 2 to 3 minutes or until it can be shaped into a ball. Place in greased bowl, turning to grease all sides. Cover with a cloth and set in a warm place free from drafts. Let rise 1 to 2 hours or until doubled in size. Grease two 8-inch square baking pans or two 9-inch, round baking pans; set aside. Punch down dough. Turn out onto a lightly floured surface. Dough will be slightly sticky. Grease your hands. Shape dough into 1-1/2-inch balls. Arrange balls in prepared pans. Cover with a cloth and set in a warm place free from drafts. Let rise about 45 minutes or until doubled in size. Preheat oven to 375F (190C). Bake 25 to 30 minutes or until golden brown. Remove from pans. Serve warm or cold. Makes 24 to 30 rolls.

Soft Pretzels

Melt Swiss cheese on top of these soft pretzels and they'll be favorites at your next party.

1 envelope active dry yeast (1 tablespoon)	**2 teaspoons salt**
1 cup warm water (105F, 40C)	**5-1/2 to 6-1/2 cups all-purpose flour**
1 egg	**1 egg yolk**
1-1/2 cups sourdough starter	**2 tablespoons water**
2 tablespoons butter or margarine, softened	**Crushed coarse salt or crushed ice cream salt**
1/4 cup sugar	

Sprinkle yeast over 1 cup warm water. Set aside to soften 5 minutes. In a large bowl, beat egg. Stir in sourdough starter, butter or margarine, sugar, salt and softened yeast mixture. Gradually stir in enough flour to make a soft dough. Turn out onto a generously floured surface. Clean and grease bowl; set aside. Knead dough 8 to 10 minutes, using flour from surface to make a stiff dough. Place in greased bowl, turning to grease all sides. Cover with a cloth and set in a warm place free from drafts. Let rise 1-1/2 to 2 hours or until doubled in size. Grease 2 large baking sheets; set aside. In a small bowl, beat egg yolk and 2 tablespoons water until smooth; set aside. Punch down dough. Divide into 3 equal portions. Divide each portion into 12 equal pieces. Roll each piece of dough between palms of your hands to make a rope about 18 inches long. Shape each rope into a pretzel by placing rope in a U-shape with ends pointing away from you. About 2 inches from ends, wrap ropes around each other at least once. Keeping rope ends separated, lift ends and twisted portion toward you. Place rope ends on top of closed end of U about 2 inches apart. Pinch ends into closed end of U to seal. Arrange on prepared baking sheets. Brush with egg yolk mixture. Sprinkle with coarse salt. Cover with a cloth and set in a warm place free from drafts. Let rise 25 minutes or until doubled in size. Preheat oven to 400F (205C). Bake 15 to 20 minutes or until golden brown. Remove from baking sheets. Cool on a rack. Makes 36 pretzels.

Sourdough Bagels

Sourdough flavor makes these bagels special.

1 envelope active dry yeast (1 tablespoon)
1/4 cup warm water (105F, 40C)
2 eggs
1 cup sourdough starter
1 teaspoon salt
2 tablespoons sugar

3 tablespoons vegetable oil
3 to 4 cups all-purpose flour
4 qts. water
2 tablespoons sugar
Butter and honey, if desired
Cream cheese and smoked salmon, if desired

Sprinkle yeast over 1/4 cup water. Set aside to soften 5 minutes. In a large bowl, beat eggs. Stir in sourdough starter, salt, 2 tablespoons sugar, oil and softened yeast mixture. Stir in enough flour to make a stiff dough. Turn out onto a lightly floured surface. Clean and lightly grease bowl; set aside. Knead dough 8 to 10 minutes or until smooth and elastic. Add more flour if necessary. Place in greased bowl, turning to grease all sides. Cover with a cloth and set in a warm place free from drafts. Let rise 1-1/2 to 2 hours or until doubled in size. Grease and flour a large baking sheet; set aside. Punch down dough and turn out onto a lightly floured surface. Knead again about 3 minutes. Divide into 12 equal pieces. Flour your hands. Shape each dough piece into a ball. Use your thumb to press a hole in center of each ball. Gently enlarge hole by turning ball in your hands as you form dough into a doughnut shape. Arrange shaped dough on prepared baking sheet. Cover with a cloth and set in a warm place free from drafts. Let rise 15 to 20 minutes. Pre-heat broiler, if necessary. In a 5-quart pot, bring 4 quarts water and 2 tablespoons sugar to a gentle boil. While water comes to a boil, broil bagels in preheated broiler 2 minutes on each side, turning with a fork. Carefully lower hot broiled bagels into gently boiling sugar-water. Boil only 4 or 5 bagels at a time. Boil 2 minutes on each side. Drain on paper towels 5 minutes. Reduce oven heat to 375F (190C). Arrange drained bagels on prepared baking sheet. Bake 25 to 35 minutes or until golden brown with a crisp crust. Remove from baking sheet. Serve hot or cold. To serve, spread with butter and drizzle with honey, or serve with cream cheese and smoked salmon. Makes 12 bagels.

Variations

Herb Bagels: Add 2 teaspoons dried leaf marjoram before adding flour.

Onion Bagels: Add 1 teaspoon dried minced onion before adding flour.

Raisin Bagels: Add 1/2 cup raisins before adding flour.

Whole-Wheat Bagels: Replace 1-1/2 cups all-purpose flour with 1-1/2 cups whole-wheat flour. Stir into sourdough mixture. Stir in enough remaining all-purpose flour to make a stiff dough.

Fry Bread

Refrigerate the dough overnight. Serve the cooked bread with jam, jelly or honey butter.

1-1/2 cups boiling water	1/2 cup warm water (105F, 40C)
1/3 cup sugar	1 cup sourdough starter
2 tablespoons butter or margarine	2 eggs, beaten
2 tablespoons shortening	7 to 8 cups all-purpose flour
2 teaspoons salt	Vegetable oil for deep-frying
2 envelopes active dry yeast (2 tablespoons)	

Pour 1-1/2 cups boiling water into a large bowl. Stir in sugar, butter or margarine, shortening and salt. Set aside to cool 10 minutes. Sprinkle yeast over 1/2 cup warm water. Set aside to soften 5 minutes. Stir sourdough starter, beaten eggs and softened yeast mixture into cooled sugar mixture. Stir in enough flour to make a soft dough. Turn out onto a lightly floured surface. Knead 3 to 5 minutes. Shape into a ball; cover with a cloth. Generously grease a plastic or glass container 3 to 4 times larger than ball of dough. Place dough in greased container. Cover with a tight-fitting lid or plastic wrap. Place in refrigerator overnight. Remove from refrigerator 2-1/2 to 3 hours before serving. Grease and flour several large baking sheets; set aside. Punch down dough and turn out onto a lightly floured surface. Roll out dough 1/3 to 1/2 inch thick. Cut into squares, rectangles or fancy shapes. Arrange cut dough on prepared baking sheets. Cover with a cloth and set in a warm place free from drafts. Let rise 1-1/2 to 2 hours or until doubled in size. Pour oil into a deep-fryer. Preheat according to manufacturer's directions. Or pour oil for deep-frying 2 inches deep into a medium skillet. Preheat oil to 365F (185C). At this temperature, a 1-inch cube of bread will turn golden brown in 50 seconds. Carefully lower dough pieces into hot oil. Cook on each side 30 to 45 seconds or until golden brown. Use a fork to turn once. Drain on paper towels. Serve hot. Makes 50 to 60 fry bread.

Cheese Rolls

An interesting way to liven up a meal.

1 envelope active dry yeast (1 tablespoon)	1/4 cup butter or margarine, softened
3/4 cup warm water (105F, 40C)	2 teaspoons salt
1 egg	4 to 5 cups all-purpose flour
1-1/2 cups sourdough starter	3/4 cup shredded sharp Cheddar cheese
1/4 cup sugar	(3 oz.)

Sprinkle yeast over water. Set aside to soften 5 minutes. In a large bowl, beat egg. Stir in sourdough starter, sugar, butter or margarine, salt, softened yeast mixture and 2 cups flour. Beat 3 to 4 minutes with electric mixer on medium speed. Stir in cheese and enough remaining flour to make a soft dough. Turn out onto a lightly floured surface. Clean and grease bowl; set aside. Knead 8 to 10 minutes or until smooth and elastic. Place in greased bowl, turning to grease all sides. Cover with a cloth and set in a warm place free from drafts. Let rise 1-1/2 to 2 hours or until doubled in size. Grease a large baking sheet; set aside. Punch down dough. Cover and let stand 10 minutes. Shape dough into 1-inch balls. Arrange on prepared baking sheet. Cover with a cloth and set in a warm place free from drafts. Let rise 1 to 2 hours or until doubled in size. Preheat oven to 375F (190C). Bake about 20 minutes or until golden brown. Remove from baking sheet. Makes 24 to 30 rolls.

Apricot Twists

This kneaded quick bread requires no rising time.

1/2 cup milk
1 cup sourdough starter
1/4 cup vegetable oil
1 teaspoon vanilla extract
3 to 4 cups all-purpose flour
1/2 teaspoon baking powder
1/4 teaspoon baking soda
1 teaspoon salt

1/3 cup sugar
1 (8-oz.) pkg. cream cheese, softened
3/4 cup apricot jam
1 cup shredded coconut
1/2 cup chopped walnuts or pecans
1/2 cup apricot jam for glaze
Shredded coconut for decoration, if desired

In a small saucepan, heat milk almost to a boil over medium heat. Do not boil. Set aside to cool 10 minutes. Generously grease a large baking sheet, set aside. In a large bowl, combine sourdough starter, cooled milk, oil and vanilla; set aside. In a medium bowl, combine 1 cup flour, baking powder, baking soda, salt and sugar. Stir into sourdough mixture. Stir in enough remaining flour to make a stiff dough. Turn out onto a lightly floured surface. Knead about 2 minutes or until smooth and elastic. Preheat oven to 375F (190C). Roll out dough to an 18'' x 10'' rectangle. Spread with softened cream cheese, then with 3/4 cup apricot jam. Sprinkle with 1 cup shredded coconut and nuts. Fold rectangle in thirds lengthwise. Use a sharp knife to cut dough crosswise into 1-inch strips. Holding strips at each end, twist in opposite directions. Arrange twisted dough on prepared baking sheet. Bake in preheated oven 20 to 25 minutes or until golden brown. In a small saucepan, heat 1/2 cup apricot jam until soft enough to brush over twists. Remove baked twists from baking sheet. Cool on a rack. While still warm, brush with warmed apricot jam. Decorate with shredded coconut, if desired. Makes about 18 twists.

Bread Sticks

Serve with soup or salad or just put them out for a snack.

1-1/2 cups warm water (105F, 40C)
1 envelope active dry yeast (1 tablespoon)
1 cup sourdough starter
3 tablespoons sugar
2 tablespoons butter or margarine, melted

2 teaspoons salt
5-1/2 to 6-1/2 cups all-purpose flour
Water for surface of dough
1 (2-1/2-oz.) can sesame seeds

Warm a large bowl. Pour water into warmed bowl. Sprinkle yeast over water. Set aside to soften 5 minutes. Stir in sourdough starter, sugar, butter or margarine, salt and 2 cups flour. Beat until smooth. Stir in enough remaining flour to make a medium-stiff dough. Turn out onto a lightly floured surface. Clean and grease bowl; set aside. Knead dough 5 to 8 minutes or until smooth. Place in greased bowl, turning to grease all sides. Cover with a cloth and set in a warm place free from drafts. Let rise 1 to 1-1/2 hours or until doubled in size. Pour sesame seeds into a 9-inch pie plate; set aside. Lightly grease a large baking sheet; set aside. Punch down dough and divide in half. On a lightly floured surface, roll out each half to a 24'' x 6'' rectangle. Cut into 1/2- to 1-inch crosswise strips. Roll each strip between your palms to make a 6- to 7-inch rope. Brush with water and roll in sesame seeds until coated. Arrange about 1 inch apart on prepared baking sheet. Cover with a cloth and set in a warm place free from drafts. Let rise 30 minutes or until slightly raised. Preheat oven to 400F (205C). Bake about 20 minutes or until browned. Remove from baking sheet. Cool on a rack. Serve warm or cold. Makes 70 to 80 bread sticks.

Pineapple Sweet Rolls

Plan your Continental breakfast around these rolls.

1/2 cup milk
1 envelope active dry yeast (1 tablespoon)
1/4 cup warm water (105F, 40C)
1/2 cup sugar
2 teaspoons ground cinnamon
1/2 teaspoon grated lemon peel
1 cup sourdough starter
1/2 cup sugar

1 teaspoon salt
1/4 cup vegetable oil
1/2 teaspoon vanilla extract
3-1/2 to 4-1/2 cups all-purpose flour
2 tablespoons butter or margarine, softened
3/4 cup well-drained crushed pineapple
Powdered Sugar Glaze, see below

Powdered Sugar Glaze:
1 tablespoon butter or margarine, melted
1-1/2 tablespoons milk

1 cup powdered sugar
1/4 teaspoon vanilla extract

In a small saucepan, heat milk almost to a boil over medium heat. Do not boil. Set aside to cool 10 minutes. Sprinkle yeast over water. Set aside to soften 5 minutes. In a small bowl, combine 1/2 cup sugar, cinnamon and lemon peel; set aside. Grease a 15-1/2" x 10-1/2" baking sheet with raised sides; set aside. In a large bowl, combine sourdough starter, cooled milk, softened yeast mixture, 1/2 cup sugar, salt, oil and vanilla. Stir in enough flour to make a medium-stiff dough. Turn out onto a lightly floured surface. Knead 8 to 10 minutes or until smooth and elastic. Add more flour if necessary. Roll out dough to a 15" x 9" rectangle. Spread with softened butter or margarine, leaving a 1-inch strip on 1 long side uncovered. Sprinkle with cinnamon mixture. Arrange drained pineapple evenly over cinnamon mixture. Beginning on covered long side, roll up jelly-roll fashion. Pinch edges to seal. Cut roll into 1-inch slices. Arrange cut side down on prepared baking sheet. Cover with a cloth and set in a warm place free from drafts. Let rise about 2 hours or until doubled in size. Preheat oven to 375F (190C). Bake 20 to 25 minutes or until golden brown. Prepare Powdered Sugar Glaze; set aside. Remove rolls from baking sheet. Arrange top side up on a rack; cool 5 minutes. Pour glaze over rolls. Serve warm or cold. Makes 15 rolls.

Powdered Sugar Glaze:
In a small bowl, blend all ingredients together. Beat until smooth.

Ginger-Cheese Spread

Delicious served with Easy Pumpkin Loaves, page 54, and Pumpkin-Mincemeat Bread, page 55.

1 (3-oz.) pkg. cream cheese, softened
2 tablespoons milk

1 teaspoon chopped crystallized ginger
2 tablespoons chopped almonds or pecans

In a small bowl, blend all ingredients. Makes 3/4 cup.

Cinnamon-Nut Rolls

Family members won't need coaxing to the breakfast table when these are on the menu.

1 envelope active dry yeast (1 tablespoon)
1/4 cup warm water (105F, 40C)
1-1/2 cups sourdough starter
3/4 cup milk
1 teaspoon vanilla extract
2 tablespoons sugar
1 teaspoon salt
1 tablespoon butter or margarine, melted

3-1/2 to 4-1/2 cups all-purpose flour
1-1/2 teaspoons ground cinnamon
1/4 cup sugar
2 tablespoons butter or margarine, softened
1/2 cup chopped walnuts or pecans
1/2 to 3/4 cup raisins, if desired
Drizzle Topping, see below

Drizzle Topping:
1-1/2 cups powdered sugar
1 to 2 tablespoons milk

3 drops vanilla extract

Sprinkle yeast over water. Set aside to soften 5 minutes. In a large bowl, combine softened yeast, sourdough starter, milk, vanilla, 2 tablespoons sugar, salt and 1 tablespoon melted butter or margarine. Stir in enough flour to make a medium-stiff dough. Turn out onto a lightly floured surface. Clean and grease bowl; set aside. Knead dough 8 to 10 minutes or until smooth and elastic. Add more flour if necessary. Dough will become softer as it is kneaded. Place in greased bowl, turning to grease all sides. Cover with a cloth and set in a warm place free from drafts. Let rise 2 hours or until doubled in size. In a small bowl, combine cinnamon and 1/4 cup sugar; set aside. Grease two 8-inch square or two 9-inch, round baking pans; set aside. Punch down dough. Turn out onto lightly floured surface. Roll out dough to a 24" x 10" rectangle. Spread softened butter or margarine over dough, leaving a 1-inch strip on 1 long side uncovered. Sprinkle buttered area evenly with cinnamon-sugar mixture. Sprinkle with chopped nuts and raisins if desired. Beginning on covered long side, roll up jelly-roll fashion. Pinch edges to seal. Cut roll into 24 slices. Arrange cut side down in prepared baking pan with sides touching. Cover with a cloth and set in a warm place free from drafts. Let rise about 1-1/2 hours or until doubled in size. Preheat oven to 400F (205C). Bake 25 to 30 minutes or until golden brown. Cool in pans 5 minutes. Prepare Drizzle Topping. Turn baked rolls out of pans onto a rack. Turn top side up. While still warm, drizzle with topping. Makes 24 rolls.

Drizzle Topping:
In a medium bowl, combine all ingredients; beat until smooth.

tip

To slice rolled dough with thread instead of a knife, place the thread crosswise under the roll. Pull the ends of the thread up and cross them over the roll. Pull tightly, cutting through the dough.

Cherry Rose Rolls   Photo on cover and page 5.

Impressive appearance matched only by their delicious flavor.

3/4 cup milk
1 envelope active dry yeast (1 tablespoon)
1/2 cup water
1 cup sourdough starter
1/2 cup butter or margarine, melted
1/2 cup granulated sugar

1-1/2 teaspoons salt
3 to 4 cups all-purpose flour
1 (21-oz.) can cherry pie filling
1 cup powdered sugar
1 teaspoon vanilla extract
1 tablespoon milk

In a small saucepan, heat 3/4 cup milk almost to a boil over medium heat. Do not boil. Set aside to cool 10 minutes. Sprinkle yeast over water. Set aside to soften 5 minutes. In a large bowl, combine sourdough starter, cooled milk, softened yeast mixture, butter or margarine, granulated sugar and salt. Stir in enough flour to make a soft dough. Turn out onto a lightly floured surface. Clean and grease bowl; set aside. Knead dough 5 to 8 minutes or until smooth and elastic. Add more flour if necessary. Place dough in greased bowl, turning to grease all sides. Cover with plastic wrap. Place in refrigerator 2 hours or overnight. Grease a large baking sheet; set aside. Punch down dough. Turn out onto a lightly floured surface. Divide dough into 24 to 30 equal pieces. Gently roll each piece between your hands to a 15-inch rope. On prepared baking sheet, loosely coil each rope, tucking end of rope under coil. Leave 2 inches between coiled ropes. Cover with a cloth and set in a warm place free from drafts. Let rise 1 to 2 hours or until doubled in size. Preheat oven to 400F (205C). Press the center of each roll with your fingers until you touch baking sheet. Make indentations about 1 inch wide. Spoon cherry pie filling into each indentation. Bake in preheated oven 12 to 15 minutes or until golden brown. Remove from baking sheet. Cool on a rack. In a small bowl, combine powdered sugar, vanilla and 1 tablespoon milk. Beat until smooth. Spoon into a pastry bag. Decorate rolls by pressing mixture through a tip with a small opening. Makes 24 to 30 rolls.

Orange-Cheese Spread

Use as a spread on your favorite bread.

2 (3-oz.) pkgs. cream cheese, softened
1/3 cup orange marmalade

1/4 teaspoon salt
1/4 teaspoon paprika

In a medium bowl, blend all ingredients. Makes about 1 cup.

tip

Yeast is sensitive to temperature changes. Set the dough in a warm place (85F, 30C) where no breezes will blow across it.

How to Make Cherry Rose Rolls

1/Shape rolls by holding one end in place and loosely coiling each rope into a circle. Tuck end under coil.

2/After coils rise, make indentations about 1-inch wide in centers. Press center of dough to baking sheet.

3/Spoon cherry pie filling into each indentation.

Orange Butterhorns

Make these for a Sunday morning surprise.

1 cup milk	**2 eggs**
1/2 cup sugar	**1 cup sourdough starter**
1-1/2 teaspoons salt	**6 to 7 cups all-purpose flour**
1/2 cup butter or margarine, melted	**1/2 cup sugar**
1 envelope active dry yeast (1 tablespoon)	**1/3 cup butter or margarine, softened**
1/4 cup warm water (105F, 40C)	**1 tablespoon grated orange peel**

In a small saucepan, heat milk almost to a boil over medium heat. Do not boil. Stir in 1/2 cup sugar, salt and 1/2 cup butter or margarine. Set aside to cool 10 minutes. Sprinkle yeast over water. Set aside to soften 5 minutes. In a large bowl, beat eggs. Stir in sourdough starter, softened yeast mixture and cooled milk mixture. Stir in 3 cups flour. Beat until smooth. Stir in enough remaining flour to make a medium-stiff dough. Cover with a cloth and set in a warm place free from drafts. Let rise 1-1/2 to 2 hours or until doubled in size. In a small bowl, combine 1/2 cup sugar, 1/3 cup soft butter or margarine and orange peel. Press with tines of a fork until blended; set aside. Grease 36 muffin cups; set aside. Punch down dough. Turn out onto a lightly floured surface. Knead about 5 minutes. Add more flour if necessary. Divide dough in half. Roll out each half to an 18" x 6" rectangle. Spread half of orange peel mixture evenly on each rectangle, leaving a 1-inch strip on 1 long side uncovered. Starting with other long side, roll up each rectangle jelly-roll fashion. Pinch edges to seal. Cut in 1-inch slices. Place cut side down in prepared muffin cups. Let rise 1-1/2 to 2 hours or until doubled in size. Preheat oven to 375F (190C). Bake 12 to 15 minutes or until golden brown. Remove from muffin cups. Serve warm. Makes 36 rolls.

How to Shape Dough Into Rolls

Rolls can be made in a variety of interesting shapes to bake in muffin tins or on a baking sheet. See page 59 for roll shapes.

Sour Cream Twists

Exceptional flavor and soft, tender texture make this a favorite.

1 teaspoon active dry yeast
1/4 cup warm water (105F, 40C)
1 cup dairy sour cream
1 egg
1 cup sourdough starter
2 tablespoons butter or margarine, melted
3 tablespoons granulated sugar

1 teaspoon salt
3 to 4 cups all-purpose flour
1/3 cup packed brown sugar
1-1/2 teaspoons ground cinnamon
2 tablespoons butter or margarine, melted
Sugar Glaze, see below

Sugar Glaze:
1-1/2 cups powdered sugar
2 tablespoons butter or margarine, softened

1 teaspoon vanilla extract
1-1/2 tablespoons hot water

Sprinkle yeast over water. Set aside to soften 5 minutes. In a small saucepan, heat sour cream until just warm. In a large bowl, beat egg. Stir in sourdough starter, softened yeast mixture, warm sour cream, 2 tablespoons melted butter or margarine, granulated sugar and salt. Stir in enough flour to make a medium-stiff dough. Turn out onto a lightly floured surface. Clean and grease bowl; set aside. Knead dough 8 to 10 minutes or until smooth. Place in greased bowl, turning to grease all sides. Cover with a cloth and set in a warm place free from drafts. Let rise 1 to 1-1/2 hours or until doubled in size. In a small bowl, combine brown sugar and cinnamon; set aside. Grease a large baking sheet; set aside. Punch down dough. Turn out onto a lightly floured surface. Roll out dough to a 24" x 12" rectangle. Brush with 2 tablespoons melted butter or margarine. Sprinkle brown sugar mixture over 1 lengthwise half of rectangle. Fold other half over brown sugar mixture. Cut folded rectangle in half lengthwise, making two 24" x 6" rectangles. Press cut edges and outside edge slightly to seal. Cut each rectangle crosswise into 1-inch strips. Holding strips at each end, twist in opposite directions. Arrange 2 inches apart on prepared baking sheet. Press ends onto sheet. Cover with a cloth and set in a warm place free from drafts. Let rise about 1 hour or until doubled in size. Preheat oven to 375F (190C). Bake 15 to 18 minutes or until golden brown. Prepare Sugar Glaze; set aside. Remove baked twists from pan. Place on a rack to cool. While warm, spread with glaze. Makes about 48 twists.

Sugar Glaze:
In a medium bowl, combine all ingredients. Beat until smooth.

tip

Use vegetable shortening to grease pans when foods are baked at 400F (205C) or higher. Butter becomes too brown.

Orange-Pecan Rolls

Contain just enough orange flavor to make them interesting.

1/2 cup milk
1 envelope active dry yeast (1 tablespoon)
1/4 cup warm water (105F, 40C)
1/2 cup sourdough starter
1/4 cup butter or margarine, melted
1/4 cup honey

1/2 teaspoon salt
1/2 teaspoon grated orange peel
2 cups whole-wheat flour
1 to 2 cups all-purpose flour
Orange-Pecan Filling, see below

Orange-Pecan Filling:
1/2 cup butter or margarine, softened
1/4 cup granulated sugar
1/4 cup packed brown sugar
1/4 cup honey

1 teaspoon orange flavoring
2 teaspoons grated orange peel
1/2 cup all-purpose flour
1/2 cup finely chopped pecans

In a small saucepan, heat milk almost to a boil over medium heat. Do not boil. Set aside to cool 10 minutes. Sprinkle yeast over water. Set aside to soften 5 minutes. Grease a large bowl; set aside. In a medium bowl, combine cooled milk, softened yeast mixture, sourdough starter, butter or margarine, honey, salt and orange peel. Stir in whole-wheat flour and 1 cup all-purpose flour. Shape into a ball. Place in prepared bowl, turning to grease all sides. Cover with a cloth and set in a warm place free from drafts. Let rise about 1-1/2 hours or until doubled in size. Prepare Orange-Pecan Filling; set aside. Generously grease a 13" x 9" baking pan; set aside. Punch down dough. Turn out onto a generously floured surface. Dough will be sticky. Flour hands. Knead dough 5 minutes or until smooth. Add more all-purpose flour if necessary. Roll out dough to a 15" x 12" rectangle. Spread evenly with filling, leaving a 1-inch strip on 1 long side uncovered. Starting with other long side, roll up jelly-roll fashion. Pinch edges to seal. Cut into fifteen 1-inch slices. Arrange cut side up in prepared baking pan. Cover with a cloth and set in a warm place free from drafts. Let rise 45 to 60 minutes or until almost doubled in size. Preheat oven to 350F (175C). Bake 35 minutes or until golden brown. Turn baked rolls out onto a serving dish. Turn top side up. Quickly scrape excess syrup from pan and spread over tops of rolls. Serve warm. To reheat, preheat oven to 350F (175C). Cover rolls with a tent of foil. Heat rolls about 20 minutes. Makes 15 rolls.

Orange-Pecan Filling:
Beat together butter or margarine, granulated sugar, brown sugar, honey, orange flavoring and orange peel. Stir in flour and pecans.

tip

Flour does not need to be sifted but should be stirred before it is measured.

Cream Cheese Puffs

Light and puffy with a cream cheese filling.

1/2 cup milk	2 eggs
1/4 cup butter or margarine	1/2 cup sourdough starter
2 tablespoons sugar	1 tablespoon grated lemon peel
1 envelope active dry yeast (1 tablespoon)	3 cups all-purpose flour
1/4 cup warm water (105F, 40C)	Cheese Filling, see below

Cheese Filling:

1 egg yolk, slightly beaten	1 tablespoon sugar
1 (8-oz.) pkg. cream cheese, softened	1 teaspoon vanilla extract

In a small saucepan, heat milk almost to a boil over medium heat. Do not boil. Stir in butter or margarine until melted. Stir in sugar. Set aside to cool 10 minutes. Sprinkle yeast over water. Set aside to soften 5 minutes. In a large bowl, beat eggs. Stir in sourdough starter, lemon peel, cooled milk mixture and softened yeast mixture. Gradually stir in all of flour until thoroughly combined. Cover bowl with a damp cloth. Refrigerate at least 2 hours. Prepare Cheese Filling; set aside. Grease a large baking sheet; set aside. Flour your hands. Punch down dough and divide into 4 equal pieces. On a lightly floured surface, roll out 1 piece of dough at a time to a 9" x 6" rectangle. Cut in half lengthwise. Cut each half into three 3-inch squares. Place 1 rounded teaspoonful of Cheese Filling in center of each square. Flour your hands again if necessary. Bring corners of square to center over filling. Pinch corners and edges together to seal. Arrange 2 inches apart on prepared baking sheet. Cover with a cloth and set in a warm place free from drafts. Let rise 25 to 35 minutes or until about doubled in size and tops feel light and tender when touched with your fingers. Preheat oven to 400F (205C). Bake 10 to 12 minutes or until golden brown. Remove from baking sheet. Serve hot. Makes 24 puffs.

Cheese Filling:
In a small bowl, combine all ingredients. Beat until smooth.

tip

Use oil to grease pans only when the food covers the entire pan. Exposed oil becomes brown and gummy and is hard to remove.

Marshmallow Balloons

You'll be surprised how good the filling is!

1/2 cup milk	2-1/2 to 3 cups all-purpose flour
1 teaspoon active dry yeast	1/2 cup packed brown sugar
1/4 cup warm water (105F, 40C)	1/2 cup granulated sugar
1 egg	2 teaspoons ground cinnamon
1 cup sourdough starter	24 large marshmallows
1/3 cup granulated sugar	1/2 cup butter or margarine, melted
1 teaspoon salt	About 3 tablespoons chopped walnuts
1/4 cup vegetable oil	or pecans

In a small saucepan, heat milk almost to a boil over medium heat. Do not boil. Set aside to cool 10 minutes. Sprinkle yeast over water. Set aside to soften 5 minutes. In a large bowl, beat egg. Stir in sourdough starter, cooled milk, softened yeast mixture, 1/3 cup granulated sugar, salt and oil. Stir in enough flour to make a soft dough. Turn out onto a lightly floured surface. Clean and grease bowl; set aside. Knead dough 5 to 8 minutes or until smooth and elastic. Place in greased bowl, turning to grease all sides. Cover with a cloth and set in a warm place free from drafts. Let rise 1 to 2 hours or until doubled in size. Generously grease 24 muffin cups; set aside. In a small bowl, combine brown sugar, 1/2 cup granulated sugar and cinnamon; set aside. Punch down dough and divide in half. Roll out until 1/4 inch thick. Cut dough into 4-inch circles. Dip each marshmallow into melted butter or margarine, then into brown sugar mixture. Place 1 dipped marshmallow on center of each dough circle. Sprinkle about 1/4 teaspoon chopped nuts over marshmallow. Loosely wrap dough around marshmallow, pinching edges tightly to seal. Dip wrapped marshmallows in remaining melted butter or margarine, then in remaining brown sugar mixture. Place 1 wrapped marshmallow seam side down in each prepared muffin cup. Cover with a cloth and set in a warm place free from drafts. Let rise about 30 minutes or until slightly raised. Preheat oven to 375F (190C). Bake 25 to 30 minutes or until golden brown. Remove from muffin cups. Serve warm or cold. Makes 24 balloons.

Sourdough Doughnuts

Raised doughnuts at their best!

1/2 cup milk
1 envelope active dry yeast (1 tablespoon)
1/4 cup warm water (105F, 40C)
1 egg
1-1/2 cups sourdough starter
1/2 teaspoon vanilla extract
2 tablespoons vegetable oil

1 teaspoon salt
1/4 cup granulated sugar
4 to 5 cups all-purpose flour
Chocolate Glaze, see below
Vegetable oil for deep-frying
Powdered sugar or granulated sugar

Chocolate Glaze:
1 cup powdered sugar
1 tablespoon unsweetened cocoa powder

2 tablespoons butter or margarine, melted
2 to 3 tablespoons hot water

In a small saucepan, heat milk almost to a boil over medium heat. Do not boil. Set aside to cool 10 minutes. Sprinkle yeast over water. Set aside to soften 5 minutes. Lightly grease and flour a large baking sheet; set aside. In a large bowl, beat egg. Stir in sourdough starter, cooled milk, softened yeast mixture, vanilla, 2 tablespoons oil, salt and 1/4 cup granulated sugar. Stir in enough flour to make a medium-stiff dough. Turn out onto a lightly floured surface. Knead 5 to 8 minutes. Add more flour if necessary. Roll out dough 1/2 inch thick. Use a doughnut cutter to cut out doughnuts. Arrange doughnuts on prepared baking sheet. Cover with a cloth and set in a warm place free from drafts. Let rise 1 hour or until doubled in size. Prepare Chocolate Glaze; set aside. Pour oil for deep-frying about 3 inches deep into a deep-fryer. Heat according to manufacturer's directions. Or pour oil about 2 inches deep into a medium skillet. Heat to 375F (190C). At this temperature a 1-inch cube of bread will turn golden brown in 40 seconds. Gently lower doughnuts 1 or 2 at a time into hot oil. Cook 1-1/2 to 2 minutes on each side or until golden brown. Drain on paper towels about 10 minutes. While still warm, dip 1 side in glaze or in powdered or granulated sugar. Cool on a rack, dipped side up. Makes 18 to 20 doughnuts.

Chocolate Glaze:
In a shallow medium bowl, combine powdered sugar, cocoa powder, butter or margarine and 2 tablespoons hot water. Add more water as needed to make a mixture thin enough to adhere to doughnuts.

tip

Oil used for deep-frying may be cooled, strained and refrigerated for reuse unless a strong-flavored food was fried in it.

Biscuits & Muffins

Biscuits and muffins will brighten an ordinary meal with new and exciting flavors while supplying good nutrition. Try light-as-a-feather Angel Biscuits, colorful Fiesta Biscuits or a variety of fruit-filled muffins, and your next meal will be a culinary delight.

When you want to make biscuits like the old-time Sourdoughs made, Old-Fashioned Sourdough Biscuits are the ones to make. Set the starter the night before. Let it stand in a warm place overnight. In the morning a pleasant sourdough aroma will greet you. Biscuits are quick to prepare from the overnight starter mixture.

Biscuits are made from slightly kneaded dough. Roll or pat out the dough on a flat surface. Use a biscuit cutter or the top of a thin-rimmed drinking glass to cut the dough. Biscuits are usually baked on an ungreased baking sheet or baking pan. But when baking sourdough biscuits, it is usually better to grease the sheet or pan lightly to prevent sticking. Cornmeal sprinkled on the baking sheet also prevents the biscuits from sticking.

Muffins are made from a batter. For the best texture, do not overmix muffin batter. As soon as the dry ingredients are moistened, pour the batter into muffin cups that have been greased or lined with paper liners. Fill the cups no more than two-thirds to three-fourths full with batter. Muffins will almost double in size as they bake.

Many of us have haunted stores looking for Sourdough English Muffins. No more! Now you can make your own. These tasty yeast-raised muffins are baked on a griddle on the stovetop.

Old-Fashioned Sourdough Biscuits

Just like the old-timers used to make.

Overnight Starter, see below
1 teaspoon cornmeal
1/4 cup vegetable oil or bacon grease,
melted
1 cup all-purpose flour

1 teaspoon baking powder
1/4 teaspoon baking soda
1 teaspoon salt
1 tablespoon sugar
1 teaspoon cornmeal, if desired

Overnight Starter:
1/2 cup sourdough starter
1 cup all-purpose flour

3/4 cup warm water (105F, 40C)

Prepare Overnight Starter the night before according to directions below. Next morning or evening, remove 1/2 cup starter. Place in a glass or plastic container or add to other starter in refrigerator. Grease a large baking sheet. Sprinkle evenly with 1 teaspoon cornmeal; set aside. Preheat oven to 250F (120C). Stir oil or bacon grease into Overnight Starter; set aside. In a small bowl, stir together flour, baking powder, baking soda, salt and sugar. Stir into sourdough mixture. Turn out onto a generously floured surface. Knead about 30 seconds. With floured hands, pat out dough 1/2 inch thick. Dip a 2- to 2-1/2-inch biscuit cutter into flour, then use to cut biscuits. Arrange biscuits on prepared baking sheet. Sprinkle tops evenly with 1 teaspoon cornmeal, if desired. Bake in preheated oven 10 minutes. Raise oven heat to 400F (205C). Bake biscuits 12 to 15 minutes longer or until lightly browned. Remove from baking sheet. Serve hot. Makes 12 to 15 biscuits.

Overnight Starter:
In a medium bowl, combine sourdough starter, flour and warm water. Set in a warm place overnight or for 24 hours.

Buttermilk Biscuits

Enjoy this Southern-style biscuit with butter and molasses.

2 cups all-purpose flour
1 teaspoon baking powder
1/2 teaspoon baking soda
1 teaspoon salt

1/2 cup butter or margarine
1 cup sourdough starter
1/2 cup buttermilk
2 tablespoons butter or margarine, melted

Lightly grease a large baking sheet; set aside. Preheat oven to 425F (220C). In a large bowl, stir together flour, baking powder, baking soda and salt. Use a pastry blender or 2 table knives to cut in 1/2 cup butter or margarine until mixture resembles coarse crumbs; set aside. In a small bowl, combine sourdough starter and buttermilk. Stir into flour mixture until thoroughly combined. Turn out onto a lightly floured surface. Gently knead dough about 30 seconds. Roll out dough 1/2 inch thick. Cut biscuits with a 2-1/2 to 3-inch biscuit cutter. On prepared baking sheet, arrange biscuits with sides touching. Brush tops with melted butter or margarine. Bake in preheated oven 12 to 15 minutes or until tops are golden brown. Remove from baking sheet. Serve hot. Makes 24 to 30 biscuits.

Ann's Sourdough Biscuits

As good as you expect biscuits to be.

1 tablespoon cornmeal
2 cups all-purpose flour
2 teaspoons baking powder
1/2 teaspoon baking soda
3/4 teaspoon salt
1 tablespoon sugar

1/2 cup shortening
1/2 cup milk
1 cup sourdough starter
1 to 2 tablespoons butter or margarine, melted
1 tablespoon cornmeal

Grease a large baking sheet. Sprinkle evenly with 1 tablespoon cornmeal; set aside. Preheat oven to 400F (205C). In a large bowl, stir together flour, baking powder, baking soda, salt and sugar. Use a pastry blender or 2 table knives to cut in shortening until mixture resembles coarse crumbs; set aside. In a small bowl, combine milk and sourdough starter. Stir into flour mixture until thoroughly combined. Turn out onto a lightly floured surface. Gently knead about 30 seconds. Dough will be very soft. Roll or pat out 1/2 inch thick. Cut biscuits with a 2- to 2-1/2-inch biscuit cutter. Arrange biscuits with sides touching on prepared baking sheet. Brush tops with melted butter or margarine. Sprinkle tops evenly with 1 tablespoon cornmeal. Bake in preheated oven 15 to 20 minutes or until tops are golden brown. Remove from pans. Serve hot. Makes 18 to 24 biscuits.

Variation

For a softer crust, omit cornmeal on baking sheet and on top of biscuits.

Refrigerator Biscuits

Prepare this dough ahead and bake fresh biscuits for the next four or five days.

1 envelope active dry yeast (1 tablespoon)
1/2 cup warm water (105F, 40C)
6 cups all-purpose flour
1 tablespoon baking powder
1 teaspoon baking soda
1-1/2 teaspoons salt

3 tablespoons sugar
1 cup shortening
1 cup sourdough starter
2 cups buttermilk
Melted butter or margarine

Grease a 10-cup plastic container with a tight-fitting lid; set aside. Sprinkle yeast over water. Set aside to soften 5 minutes. In a large bowl, stir together flour, baking powder, baking soda, salt and sugar. Use a pastry blender or 2 table knives to cut in shortening until mixture resembles coarse crumbs; set aside. In a medium bowl, combine sourdough starter, buttermilk and softened yeast mixture. Stir into flour mixture until dry ingredients are just moistened. Turn into prepared plastic container. Cover tightly. Store in refrigerator 4 to 5 days, using dough to make biscuits as desired. **To bake biscuits:** Lightly grease a baking pan. Size of pan is determined by number of biscuits you make. Set pan aside. Pinch off about 1/4 cup dough for each biscuit. On a generously floured surface, roll or pat out dough 1/2 inch thick. Cut biscuits with a 2- to 2-1/2-inch biscuit cutter. Arrange in prepared baking pan with sides of biscuits touching. Let stand 5 minutes. Brush tops of biscuits with melted butter or margarine. Preheat oven to 400F (205C). Bake 15 to 18 minutes or until tops are golden brown. Remove from pan. Serve hot. Makes 80 to 90 biscuits.

Onion Biscuits

Spoon creamed tuna or Chicken à la King, page 152, over these savory biscuits.

1 tablespoon butter or margarine	**1/2 teaspoon celery seeds**
1/4 cup finely chopped onion	**1/2 cup shortening**
2 cups all-purpose flour	**1 egg**
2 teaspoons baking powder	**1 cup sourdough starter**
1/2 teaspoon baking soda	**1 tablespoon butter or margarine, melted**
1/2 teaspoon salt	

Grease a 13" x 9" baking pan; set aside. In a small skillet, melt 1 tablespoon butter or margarine. Add onion. Sauté onion until tender; set aside. In a large bowl, stir together flour, baking powder, baking soda, salt and celery seeds. Use a pastry blender or 2 table knives to cut in shortening until mixture resembles coarse crumbs; set aside. In a small bowl, beat egg. Stir in sourdough starter and sautéed onion. Stir into flour mixture until thoroughly combined. Turn out onto a lightly floured surface. Preheat oven to 425F (220C). Gently knead dough about 30 seconds. Roll out dough 1/2 inch thick. Cut biscuits with a 2- to 2-1/2-inch biscuit cutter. Arrange biscuits in prepared baking pan with sides of biscuits touching. Brush tops with melted butter or margarine. Bake in preheated oven 12 to 15 minutes or until tops are golden brown. Remove from baking pan. Serve hot. Makes 18 to 24 biscuits.

Whole-Wheat Herb Biscuits

An extra special biscuit—serve with salad or fruit.

1/2 cup whole-wheat flour	**1 teaspoon Italian seasoning**
1/2 cup all-purpose flour	**1 teaspoon dried minced onion**
1-1/2 teaspoons baking powder	**1/4 cup shortening**
1/4 teaspoon baking soda	**1/2 cup sourdough starter**
1/2 teaspoon sugar	**1/4 cup milk**
1/2 teaspoon salt	**1 tablespoon butter or margarine, melted**

Grease a medium baking sheet; set aside. Preheat oven to 425F (220C). In a large bowl, stir together whole-wheat flour, all-purpose flour, baking powder, baking soda, sugar, salt, Italian seasoning and dried onion. Use a pastry blender or 2 table knives to cut in shortening until mixture resembles coarse crumbs; set aside. In a medium bowl, combine sourdough starter and milk. Stir into flour mixture until dry ingredients are just moistened. Turn out onto a lightly floured surface. Gently knead dough about 30 seconds. Dough will be soft. Roll or pat out dough 1/2 inch thick. Cut biscuits with a 2- to 2-1/2-inch biscuit cutter. Arrange on prepared baking sheet with sides of biscuits touching. Brush tops with melted butter or margarine. Bake in preheated oven 12 to 15 minutes or until tops are golden brown. Remove from baking sheet. Serve hot. Makes 12 to 14 biscuits.

Pecan Drop Biscuits

These delightful biscuits are easy to prepare.

1/2 teaspoon ground cinnamon	3 tablespoons sugar
2 tablespoons sugar	1/3 cup shortening
1-1/4 cups all-purpose flour	1/2 cup finely chopped pecans
1 teaspoon baking powder	1 egg
1/2 teaspoon baking soda	1 cup sourdough starter
1/2 teaspoon salt	

Grease a large baking sheet; set aside. In a small bowl, combine cinnamon and 2 tablespoons sugar; set aside. Preheat oven to 425F (220C). In a large bowl, stir together flour, baking powder, baking soda, salt and 3 tablespoons sugar. Use a pastry blender or 2 table knives to cut in shortening until mixture resembles coarse crumbs. Stir in pecans; set aside. In a small bowl, beat egg. Stir in sourdough starter. Stir into flour mixture until thoroughly combined. Drop by heaping teaspoonfuls onto prepared baking sheet. Sprinkle cinnamon-sugar mixture over biscuits. Bake in preheated oven 10 to 12 minutes or until tops are golden brown. Remove from baking sheet. Serve hot. Makes 24 to 30 biscuits.

Variation

Omit cinnamon-sugar topping. Serve open-face with Chicken à la King, page 152.

Angel Biscuits   Photo on page 92.

This cross between a roll and a biscuit is light as a feather. Honest!

1 teaspoon active dry yeast	1 teaspoon sugar
2 tablespoons warm water (105F, 40C)	1/4 cup shortening
1-1/4 to 1-1/2 cups all-purpose flour	1 cup sourdough starter
1 teaspoon baking powder	1/4 cup butter or margarine, melted
1/2 teaspoon salt	

In a small bowl, sprinkle yeast over water. Set aside to soften 5 minutes. For biscuits with crisp sides, grease a large baking sheet. For softer biscuits, grease a 13'' x 9'' baking pan; set aside. In a large bowl, stir together 1-1/4 cups flour, baking powder, salt and sugar. Use a pastry blender or 2 table knives to cut in shortening until mixture resembles coarse crumbs. Use a fork to stir in sourdough starter and softened yeast mixture until thoroughly combined. Turn out onto a lightly floured surface. Gently knead about 1 minute. Add more flour if necessary. Roll out dough 1/2 inch thick. Cut biscuits with a 2- to 2-1/2-inch biscuit cutter. Dip both sides of biscuits in melted butter or margarine. Arrange 1 inch apart on prepared baking sheet or in prepared pan with sides of biscuits touching. Cover with a cloth and set in a warm place free from drafts. Let rise 1 hour or until about doubled in size. Preheat oven to 400F (205C). Bake 20 to 25 minutes or until tops are golden brown. Remove from baking sheet or pan. Serve hot. Makes 18 to 20 biscuits.

How to Make Pecan Drop Biscuits

1/Use a pastry blender or 2 table knives to cut in shortening until mixture resembles coarse crumbs.

2/Stir in pecans, starter and eggs. Drop by heaping teaspoonfuls onto prepared baking sheet.

Cinnamon Biscuits

Butter these biscuits while they are hot and serve them with your morning coffee.

1-1/2 cups all-purpose flour
2 teaspoons baking powder
1/2 teaspoon baking soda
1/2 teaspoon salt
1/4 cup packed brown sugar
1 teaspoon ground cinnamon

1/4 teaspoon ground nutmeg
1/2 cup shortening
1/2 cup raisins
1 cup sourdough starter
2 tablespoons butter or margarine, melted

Grease a 12" x 7-1/2" baking pan; set aside. Preheat oven to 425F (220C). In a large bowl, stir together flour, baking powder, baking soda, salt, brown sugar, cinnamon and nutmeg. Use a pastry blender or 2 table knives to cut in shortening until mixture resembles coarse crumbs. Add raisins and sourdough starter. Stir until blended. Turn out onto a lightly floured surface. Knead dough about 30 seconds. Roll out dough 1/2 inch thick. Cut biscuits with a 2- to 2-1/2-inch biscuit cutter. Arrange in prepared baking pan with sides of biscuits touching. Brush tops of biscuits with melted butter or margarine. Bake in preheated oven 12 to 15 minutes or until tops are golden brown. Remove from pan. Serve hot. Makes 20 to 22 biscuits.

Fiesta Biscuits

Colorful and tasty. Serve with a salad luncheon for a special treat.

1/2 cup milk
1 teaspoon active dry yeast
2 tablespoons warm water (105F, 40C)
2-1/2 to 3 cups all-purpose flour
2 teaspoons baking powder
1/2 teaspoon baking soda
1/2 teaspoon salt

1/2 cup shortening
1 cup sourdough starter
1/2 to 2/3 cup shredded Longhorn cheese
   (2 to 3 oz.)
2 tablespoons chopped canned pimiento
2 tablespoons finely chopped green pepper
2 tablespoons butter or margarine, melted

In a small saucepan, heat milk almost to a boil over medium heat. Do not boil. Set aside to cool 10 minutes. In a small bowl, sprinkle yeast over water. Set aside to soften 5 minutes. For biscuits with crisp sides, grease a large baking sheet. For softer biscuits, grease a 13" x 9" baking pan; set aside. Preheat oven to 400F (205C). In a large bowl, stir together flour, baking powder, baking soda and salt. Use a pastry blender or 2 table knives to cut in shortening until mixture resembles coarse crumbs; set aside. In a medium bowl, combine cooled milk, softened yeast mixture, sourdough starter, cheese, pimiento and green pepper. Stir into flour mixture until thoroughly combined. Turn out onto a lightly floured surface. Knead dough about 30 seconds. Roll out dough 1/2 inch thick. Cut biscuits with a 2- to 2-1/2-inch biscuit cutter. Arrange 1 inch apart on prepared baking sheet or in prepared baking pan with sides of biscuits touching. Brush tops with melted butter or margarine. Bake in preheated oven 20 to 25 minutes or until tops are golden brown. Remove from baking sheet or pan. Serve hot. Makes 24 to 36 biscuits.

Variation

For lighter biscuits, cover unbaked biscuits with a cloth and set in a warm place free from drafts. Let rise 50 to 60 minutes or until about doubled in size. Bake as directed above.

Cottage Cheese Muffins

Perfect complement to a colorful fruit salad.

2 cups all-purpose flour
1-1/2 teaspoons baking powder
1/2 teaspoon baking soda
1/2 teaspoon salt
1/4 cup sugar
2 eggs

1/2 cup sourdough starter
1/4 cup vegetable oil
1/2 cup milk
1 cup creamed cottage cheese (8 oz.)
1 tablespoon lemon peel

Grease 14 muffin cups or line with paper liners; set aside. Preheat oven to 400F (205C). In a large bowl, stir together flour, baking powder, baking soda, salt and sugar; set aside. In a medium bowl, beat eggs. Stir in sourdough starter, oil, milk, cottage cheese and lemon peel. Add to flour mixture. Stir with a fork until dry ingredients are just moistened. Fill prepared muffin cups 2/3 to 3/4 full with batter. Bake in preheated oven 20 to 25 minutes or until golden brown. Remove from muffin cups. Serve hot. Makes 12 to 14 muffins.

Mexican Muffins

Colorful Mexican-style muffins add an exotic touch to a weekend brunch.

2 slices bacon
1-3/4 cups all-purpose flour
2 teaspoons baking powder
1/8 teaspoon baking soda
1/4 teaspoon salt
2 tablespoons sugar
1/8 teaspoon chili powder
1/2 cup shredded Cheddar cheese (2 oz.)

1 egg
1/2 cup sourdough starter
1/3 cup milk
1 cup cream-style corn
1/4 cup vegetable oil
1 tablespoon canned chopped green chilies
2 tablespoons chopped canned pimiento

In a medium skillet, cook bacon over medium heat until crisp. Drain on paper towels. Crumble and set aside. Grease 18 muffin cups or line with paper liners; set aside. Preheat oven to 400F (205C). In a large bowl, stir together flour, baking powder, baking soda, salt, sugar and chili powder. Stir in cheese; set aside. In a medium bowl, beat egg. Stir in sourdough starter, milk, corn, oil, chilies and pimiento. Add to flour mixture. Stir with a fork until dry ingredients are just moistened. Fold in crumbled bacon. Fill prepared muffin cups 2/3 to 3/4 full with batter. Bake in preheated oven 20 to 25 minutes or until golden brown. Remove from muffin cups. Serve hot. Makes 18 muffins.

Bacon & Cheese Muffins

Just drink a glass of orange juice and eat one of these muffins and your breakfast is complete.

4 slices bacon
1-1/2 cups all-purpose flour
2 teaspoons baking powder
1/4 teaspoon baking soda
1/2 teaspoon salt
1/4 cup sugar

1/2 cup shredded Cheddar cheese (2 oz.)
1 egg
1/2 cup sourdough starter
2/3 cup milk
1/3 cup vegetable oil or bacon drippings

In a medium skillet, cook bacon over medium heat until crisp. Reserve bacon drippings, if desired. Drain cooked bacon on paper towels. Crumble and set aside. Grease 12 muffin cups or line with paper liners; set aside. Preheat oven to 400F (205C). In a large bowl, stir together flour, baking powder, baking soda, salt and sugar. Stir in cheese; set aside. In a medium bowl, beat egg. Stir in sourdough starter, milk and oil or drippings. Add to flour mixture. Stir with a fork until dry ingredients and just moistened. Fold in crumbled bacon. Fill prepared muffin cups 2/3 to 3/4 full with batter. Bake in preheated oven 20 to 25 minutes or until golden brown. Remove from muffin cups. Serve hot. Makes 12 muffins.

Pruffins   Photo on page 99.

Who wants to eat prune muffins? Call them Pruffins and your family will love them.

1 cup whole-bran cereal	**1 cup whole-wheat flour**
3/4 cup milk	**2 teaspoons baking powder**
1 egg, beaten	**1/2 teaspoon salt**
1/4 cup vegetable oil	**2 tablespoons butter or margarine, melted**
1/2 cup sourdough starter	**1/4 cup packed brown sugar**
1/4 cup honey or 1/2 cup sugar	**12 pitted prunes**

Grease 12 muffin cups or line with paper liners; set aside. Preheat oven to 375F (190C). In a large bowl, combine cereal and milk. Let stand about 15 minutes or until most of milk is absorbed. Beat in egg, oil, sourdough starter and honey or sugar. In a small bowl, stir together flour, baking powder and salt. Stir into sourdough mixture until dry ingredients are just moistened. Spoon 1/2 teaspoon melted butter or margarine into each prepared muffin cup. Add 1 teaspoon brown sugar and 1 prune to each muffin cup. Fill cups 2/3 to 3/4 full with batter. Bake 18 to 25 minutes or until tops are golden brown. Place a rack over top of cooked muffins. Invert rack and muffin pan. Remove pan. Makes 18 to 25 muffins.

Bran Muffins

For muffin lovers of all ages.

1 egg	**1-1/2 cups whole-wheat flour**
1/2 cup sourdough starter	**3/4 teaspoon baking soda**
1/4 cup honey	**1/2 teaspoon salt**
1/4 cup vegetable oil	**1/2 cup whole-bran cereal**
1/2 cup milk	**1/2 cup raisins**

Grease 12 muffin cups or line with paper liners; set aside. Preheat oven to 400F (205C). In a medium bowl, beat egg. Stir in sourdough starter, honey, oil and milk; set aside. In another medium bowl, stir together flour, baking soda and salt. Stir into sourdough mixture until dry ingredients are just moistened. Fold in cereal and raisins. Fill prepared muffin cups 2/3 to 3/4 full with batter. Bake 18 to 20 minutes or until a wooden pick inserted in center comes out clean. Makes 10 to 12 muffins.

Variation

Substitute 1/2 cup sugar for honey; substitute 1/2 teaspoon baking soda and 1 teaspoon baking powder for 3/4 teaspoon baking soda.

How to Make Pruffins

1/Spoon melted butter or margarine and brown sugar in bottom of each muffin cup. Add a pitted prune.

2/Fill each muffin cup 2/3 to 3/4 full with batter.

Cornmeal Muffins

Serve piping hot with chili and beans.

1 cup all-purpose flour	**1 teaspoon sugar**
1 cup cornmeal	**1 egg**
2 teaspoons baking powder	**1/2 cup sourdough starter**
1/4 teaspoon baking soda	**1/4 cup vegetable oil**
1 teaspoon salt	**1 cup milk**

Grease 16 muffin cups or line with paper liners; set aside. Preheat oven to 400F (205C). In a large bowl, stir together flour, cornmeal, baking powder, baking soda, salt and sugar; set aside. In a medium bowl, beat egg. Stir in sourdough starter, oil and milk. Add to flour mixture. Stir with a fork until dry ingredients are just moistened. Fill prepared muffin cups 2/3 to 3/4 full with batter. Bake 15 to 20 minutes or until golden brown. Remove from muffin cups. Serve hot. Makes 12 to 16 muffins.

Lemon-Nut Muffins

Frozen lemonade concentrate is used in the batter and as a topping.

1-1/2 cups all-purpose flour
2 teaspoons baking powder
1/8 teaspoon baking soda
1/2 teaspoon salt
1/4 cup sugar
1 egg
1/4 cup milk

2 teaspoons grated lemon peel
1/2 cup sourdough starter
1/3 cup thawed frozen lemonade concentrate
1/3 cup vegetable oil
1/2 cup chopped walnuts or pecans
Thawed frozen lemonade concentrate
About 2 teaspoons sugar

Grease 14 muffin cups or line with paper liners; set aside. Preheat oven to 400F (205C). In a large bowl, stir together flour, baking powder, baking soda, salt and 1/4 cup sugar; set aside. In a medium bowl, beat egg. Stir in milk and lemon peel. Stir in sourdough starter, 1/3 cup lemonade concentrate, oil and nuts. Add to flour mixture. Stir with a fork until dry ingredients are just moistened. Fill prepared muffin cups 2/3 to 3/4 full with batter. Bake in preheated oven 20 to 25 minutes or until golden brown. Remove from muffin cups. While still warm, brush tops with lemonade concentrate. Sprinkle lightly with sugar. Makes 12 to 14 muffins.

Date-Nut Muffins

Superb way to combine dates and nuts.

1-1/2 cups all-purpose flour
2 teaspoons baking powder
1/2 teaspoon salt
1/2 cup sugar
1 egg

1/2 cup sourdough starter
1/3 cup butter or margarine, melted
1 cup milk
1 cup chopped dates
1/2 cup chopped walnuts or pecans

Grease 14 muffin cups or line with paper liners. Preheat oven to 375F (190C). In a large bowl, stir together flour, baking powder, salt and sugar; set aside. In a medium bowl, beat egg. Stir in sourdough starter, butter or margarine and milk. Add to flour mixture. Stir with a fork until dry ingredients are just moistened. Fold in dates and nuts. Fill prepared muffin cups 2/3 to 3/4 full with batter. Bake in preheated oven 20 to 25 minutes or until golden brown. Remove from muffin cups. Serve hot. Makes 12 to 14 muffins.

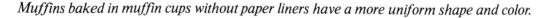

tip

Muffins baked in muffin cups without paper liners have a more uniform shape and color.

Apple-Nut Muffins

Thank you, Johnny Appleseed!

1/2 cup sugar
1/3 cup shortening
1 egg
1/2 cup sourdough starter
2/3 cup milk
1 cup finely shredded unpeeled apple

1/2 cup chopped walnuts or pecans
1-1/2 cups all-purpose flour
2-1/2 teaspoons baking powder
1/2 teaspoon salt
1 teaspoon ground cinnamon

Grease 16 muffin cups or line with paper liners; set aside. Preheat oven to 400F (205C). In a medium bowl, cream sugar and shortening. Add egg, sourdough starter and milk. Beat until thoroughly combined. Fold in apple and nuts; set aside. In a small bowl, stir together flour, baking powder, salt and cinnamon. Add to sourdough mixture. Stir with a fork until dry ingredients are just moistened. Fill prepared muffin cups 2/3 to 3/4 full with batter. Bake in preheated oven 20 to 25 minutes or until golden brown. Remove from muffin cups. Serve hot. Makes 12 to 16 muffins.

Pumpkin Muffins

Pumpkin and spice. Makes you think of pumpkin pie.

1-1/2 cups all-purpose flour
2 teaspoons baking powder
1/2 teaspoon salt
1/2 cup sugar
3/4 teaspoon ground cinnamon
1/2 teaspoon ground nutmeg
1/4 cup butter or margarine

1 egg
1/2 cup sourdough starter
1/2 cup milk
1/2 cup canned pumpkin
1/2 cup raisins
About 2 tablespoons granulated sugar

Grease 14 muffin cups or line with paper liners; set aside. Preheat oven to 400F (205C). In a large bowl, stir together flour, baking powder, salt, 1/2 cup sugar, cinnamon and nutmeg. Use a pastry blender or 2 table knives to cut in butter or margarine until mixture resembles fine crumbs; set aside. In a medium bowl, beat egg. Stir in sourdough starter, milk, pumpkin and raisins. Add to flour mixture. Stir with a fork until dry ingredients are just moistened. Fill prepared muffin cups 2/3 to 3/4 full with batter. Sprinkle 1/8 to 1/4 teaspoon sugar over each muffin. Bake 25 to 30 minutes or until golden brown. Remove from muffin cups. Serve hot. Makes 12 to 14 muffins.

Cranberry-Orange Muffins

Serve this muffin when you want to add color to a meal.

1-1/2 cups all-purpose flour
2 teaspoons baking powder
1/2 teaspoon salt
1/4 cup sugar
1 egg
1/2 cup sourdough starter

3/4 cup orange juice
1/3 cup vegetable oil
1 tablespoon grated orange peel
3/4 cup canned whole cranberry sauce
1/2 cup chopped walnuts or pecans

Grease 18 muffin cups or line with paper liners; set aside. Preheat oven to 400F (205C). In a large bowl, stir together flour, baking powder, salt and sugar; set aside. In a medium bowl, beat egg. Stir in sourdough starter, orange juice, oil and orange peel. Add to flour mixture. Stir with a fork until dry ingredients are just moistened. Fold in cranberry sauce and nuts. Fill prepared muffin cups 2/3 to 3/4 full with batter. Bake in preheated oven 20 to 25 minutes or until tops are golden brown. Remove from muffin cups. Serve hot. Makes 18 muffins.

Variation

Dip tops of warm muffins in melted butter or margarine, then in granulated sugar.

Granola-Apple Muffins

How could anything so good be so good for you?

1 egg
1/2 cup sourdough starter
1/2 cup milk
1/4 cup vegetable oil
1/4 cup honey
1/2 cup applesauce

1-1/2 cups whole-wheat flour
1-1/2 teaspoons baking powder
1/2 teaspoon baking soda
1/2 teaspoon salt
1 cup granola cereal

Grease 14 muffin cups or line with paper liners; set aside. Preheat oven to 400F (205C). In a medium bowl, beat egg. Stir in sourdough starter, milk, oil, honey and applesauce; set aside. In a medium bowl, stir together flour, baking powder, baking soda and salt. Stir into sourdough mixture until dry ingredients are just moistened. Fold in granola. Fill prepared muffin cups 2/3 to 3/4 full with batter. Bake in preheated oven 15 to 22 minutes or until a wooden pick inserted in center comes out clean. Remove from muffin cups. Serve hot. Makes 12 to 14 muffins.

Top, Angel Biscuits, page 84; bottom, Cranberry-Orange Muffins

Raisin-Rich Muffins

Different and rich.

3/4 cup whole-wheat flour
1-1/2 cups all-purpose flour
1-1/2 teaspoons baking powder
1/4 teaspoon baking soda
1 teaspoon salt
1/2 cup sugar

2 eggs
1/2 cup sourdough starter
1/2 cup vegetable oil
3/4 cup evaporated milk
1 cup raisins

Grease 24 muffin cups or line with paper liners; set aside. Preheat oven to 425F (220C). In a large bowl, stir together whole-wheat flour, all-purpose flour, baking powder, baking soda, salt and sugar; set aside. In a medium bowl, beat eggs. Stir in sourdough starter, oil and milk. Add to flour mixture. Stir with a fork until dry ingredients are just moistened. Fold in raisins. Fill prepared muffin cups 2/3 to 3/4 full with batter. Bake in preheated oven 20 to 25 minutes or until golden brown. Remove from muffin cups. Serve hot. Makes 18 to 24 muffins.

Pineapple Muffins

Pineapple Glaze settles into each muffin as it bakes.

1 (16-oz.) can crushed pineapple
Pineapple Glaze, see below
1 cup all-purpose flour
2 teaspoons baking powder
1/4 teaspoon baking soda
1/2 teaspoon salt
3/4 cup whole-bran cereal

1/3 cup packed brown sugar
1/4 teaspoon ground cinnamon
1 egg
1/2 cup sourdough starter
1/3 cup vegetable oil
1/2 cup milk

Pineapple Glaze:
2 tablespoons sugar
1 tablespoon cornstarch

Reserved pineapple and juice

Grease 18 muffin cups or line with paper liners; set aside. Drain pineapple, reserving juice. Reserve half of drained pineapple for muffins. Prepare Pineapple Glaze with remaining drained pineapple and reserved juice; set aside. Preheat oven to 400F (205C). In a large bowl, stir together flour, baking powder, baking soda, salt, cereal, brown sugar and cinnamon; set aside. In a medium bowl, beat egg. Stir in sourdough starter, oil, milk and reserved drained pineapple. Add to flour mixture. Stir with a fork until dry ingredients are just moistened. Fill prepared muffin cups 2/3 to 3/4 full with batter. Top each with 1 rounded teaspoonful of Pineapple Glaze. Bake in preheated oven 20 to 25 minutes or until golden brown. Remove from muffin cups. Serve hot. Makes 14 to 18 muffins.

Pineapple Glaze:
In a small saucepan, combine sugar and cornstarch. Stir in pineapple and juice. Stirring constantly, bring to a boil over medium heat. Stir and boil 2 minutes or until thickened. Set aside to cool.

Pineapple-Macadamia Muffins

Inspired by a visit to Hawaii. Cashews can also be used as a topping.

1-1/2 cups all-purpose flour
2 teaspoons baking powder
1/4 teaspoon baking soda
3/4 teaspoon salt
1/2 cup sugar
1/2 teaspoon ground cinnamon
1 cup finely shredded coconut

1 cup crushed pineapple with juice
About 1/2 cup milk
1 egg
1/2 cup sourdough starter
1/3 cup vegetable oil
About 1/3 cup finely chopped macadamia nuts

Grease 18 muffin cups or line with paper liners; set aside. Preheat oven to 375F (190C). In a large bowl, stir together flour, baking powder, baking soda, salt, sugar and cinnamon. Stir in coconut; set aside. Drain juice from pineapple into a 1-cup measure. Reserve drained pineapple. Add milk to pineapple juice to make 3/4 cup; set aside. In a medium bowl, beat egg. Stir in juice mixture, reserved pineapple, sourdough starter and oil. Add to flour mixture. Stir with a fork until dry ingredients are just moistened. Fill prepared muffin cups 2/3 to 3/4 full with batter. Sprinkle about 1 teaspoon macadamia nuts over top of each muffin. Bake in preheated oven 18 to 20 minutes or until golden brown. Remove from muffin cups. Serve hot. Makes 15 to 18 muffins.

Pineapple-Cheese Muffins

Pineapple and Cheddar cheese make a delightfully different blend of flavors.

1-3/4 cups all-purpose flour
2 teaspoons baking powder
1/4 teaspoon baking soda
1/2 teaspoon salt
1/2 cup sugar
3/4 cup shredded Cheddar cheese (3 oz.)

1 egg
1/2 cup sourdough starter
1/3 cup vegetable oil
1 cup crushed pineapple with juice
1/2 cup milk

Grease 18 muffin cups or line with paper liners; set aside. Preheat oven to 375F (190C). In a large bowl, stir together flour, baking powder, baking soda, salt and sugar. Stir in cheese until evenly distributed; set aside. In a medium bowl, beat egg. Stir in sourdough starter, oil, pineapple with juice and milk. Add to flour mixture. Stir with a fork until dry ingredients are just moistened. Fill prepared muffin cups 2/3 to 3/4 full with batter. Bake in preheated oven 18 to 20 minutes or until golden brown. Remove from muffin cups. Serve hot. Makes 15 to 18 muffins.

tip

Grate cheese just before it is added to a recipe. Cheese packs down as it sits.

Tropical Muffins

A good way to use up ripe bananas.

2 cups all-purpose flour	2 eggs
1-1/2 teaspoons baking powder	1 cup sourdough starter
1/2 teaspoon baking soda	1/2 cup vegetable oil
3/4 teaspoon salt	1 cup mashed ripe bananas
1/2 cup sugar	1/3 cup orange juice
1/2 cup shredded coconut	1 teaspoon grated orange peel

Lightly grease 18 muffin cups or line with paper liners; set aside. Preheat oven to 375F (190C). In a large bowl, stir together flour, baking powder, baking soda, salt and sugar. Stir in coconut. Make a well in center; set aside. In a medium bowl, beat eggs. Stir in sourdough starter, oil, bananas, orange juice and orange peel. Pour into well in flour mixture. Stir with a fork until dry ingredients are just moistened. Fill prepared muffin cups 2/3 to 3/4 full with batter. Bake in preheated oven 25 to 30 minutes or until golden brown. Remove from muffin cups. Serve hot. Makes 16 to 18 muffins.

Oatmeal Muffins

Nutritious and filling.

1 cup rolled oats	1 cup all-purpose flour
1 cup milk	1-1/2 teaspoons baking powder
1/2 cup sourdough starter	1/4 teaspoon baking soda
1/3 cup vegetable oil	1/2 teaspoon salt
1 egg, beaten	1/2 cup packed brown sugar
1/2 cup raisins, if desired	

In a medium bowl, combine rolled oats and milk. Set aside to soak 1 hour. Grease 14 muffin cups or line with paper liners; set aside. Preheat oven to 400F (205C). Stir sourdough starter, oil, egg and raisins, if desired, into soaked oats; set aside. In a large bowl, stir together flour, baking powder, baking soda, salt and brown sugar. Add oats mixture. Stir with a fork until dry ingredients are just moistened. Fill prepared muffin cups 2/3 to 3/4 full with batter. Bake in preheated oven 20 to 25 minutes or until golden brown. Remove from muffin cups. Serve hot. Makes 12 to 14 muffins.

How to Make Tropical Muffins

1/Make a well in center of dry ingredients. Pour all liquids into well.

2/Stir until dry ingredients are just moistened. Fill prepared muffin cups 2/3 to 3/4 full with batter.

Orange-Chip Muffins

Orange flavor and chocolate pieces make a glorious dessert muffin.

1-1/2 cups all-purpose flour	**1/2 cup sourdough starter**
2 teaspoons baking powder	**1/2 cup orange juice**
1/4 teaspoon baking soda	**2 teaspoons grated orange peel**
1/2 teaspoon salt	**1/4 cup milk**
1/2 cup sugar	**1/3 cup vegetable oil**
1 egg	**3/4 cup semisweet chocolate pieces**

Grease 14 muffin cups or line with paper liners; set aside. Preheat oven to 375F (190C). In a large bowl, stir together flour, baking powder, baking soda, salt and sugar; set aside. In a small bowl, beat egg. Stir in sourdough starter, orange juice, orange peel, milk and oil. Add to flour mixture. Stir with a fork until dry ingredients are just moistened. Fold in chocolate pieces. Fill prepared muffin cups 2/3 to 3/4 full with batter. Bake in preheated oven 18 to 20 minutes or until golden brown. Remove from muffin cups. Serve hot. Makes 12 to 14 muffins.

English Muffins

Split, toast and serve with butter.

1 envelope active dry yeast (1 tablespoon)
1/4 cup warm water (105F, 40C)
2 tablespoons yellow cornmeal
2-3/4 cups all-purpose flour
1/4 cup yellow cornmeal

1 teaspoon baking soda
1 teaspoon salt
1 cup sourdough starter
3/4 cup buttermilk

Sprinkle yeast over water. Set aside to soften 5 minutes. Cover a large baking sheet with waxed paper. Sprinkle with 1 tablespoon cornmeal; set aside. In a large bowl, stir together flour, 1/4 cup cornmeal, baking soda and salt; set aside. In a medium bowl, combine sourdough starter, buttermilk and softened yeast mixture. Stir into flour mixture until blended. Turn out onto a lightly floured surface. Knead 5 to 8 minutes or until smooth and elastic. Add more flour if necessary. Roll out dough 3/8 to 1/2 inch thick. Cut muffins with a 3-inch biscuit cutter or top of a 3-inch-wide drinking glass. Arrange muffins on prepared baking sheet. Sprinkle with remaining tablespoon cornmeal. Cover with a cloth and set in a warm place free from drafts. Let rise 45 minutes or until about doubled in size. Preheat griddle according to manufacturer's directions. Or place griddle over medium to medium-high heat until a drop of water bounces over surface. Lightly grease griddle. Turning often, cook raised muffins on medium-hot griddle about 30 minutes. Cool on a rack. Serve warm or cold. Makes 12 to 14 muffins.

Variation

After cooking 15 to 20 minutes, split muffins and place cut side down on griddle. Turning often, cook 3 to 4 minutes until lightly browned.

tip
_____

If you don't have a biscuit cutter, use the open end of a small tuna can or an 8-ounce tomato sauce can.

Top right, Onion-Rye Bread, page 37; lower left, Pruffins, page 88.

Pancakes & Waffles

When preparing pancakes, be sure to heat the griddle or skillet to 375 to 400F (190 to 205C). Temperature can be tested with a few drops of cold water sprinkled on the hot pan. If the drops bounce and sputter, the temperature is right. Before pouring on the batter, grease the cooking surface with shortening or non-stick spray. Cook one small pancake to be sure the temperature is correct and the cooking surface is properly greased.

Old-Fashioned Sourdough Pancakes are made with an overnight starter mixture and have a different texture than other pancakes. Gluten in the batter becomes more elastic because it stands for 10 to 12 hours. If a lighter texture is desired, separate the eggs and add the yolks to the mixture. Then beat the whites to the soft-peak stage and gently fold them into the batter before cooking. The texture will still be more firm than ordinary pancakes, but sourdough pancakes are not ordinary! Cook these sourdough pancakes a little longer than you would cook other pancakes. Wait until bubbles form and break on top before turning them.

Quick Sourdough Pancakes are light and airy and can be made at the last minute. Cook them on a hot griddle until the edges become dry and the bottom is golden brown. Turn them over and lightly brown the other side. You can make seven variations from this one recipe. Blueberry Pancakes are easy to prepare. Just fold one cup of fresh, frozen or canned blueberries into the batter. Banana Pancakes contain sliced, diced or mashed banana. Serve them with Banana Sauce for a real banana treat. Some of the variations can be combined, giving you even more variations.

Basic Sourdough Waffles will almost melt in your mouth. Apricot-Pecan Waffles are made from the basic recipe, then have orange peel and pecans folded into the batter. Serve them with Apricot Sauce or Apricot Syrup.

Quick Sourdough Pancakes

Light and airy. Make them at the last minute.

1-1/4 cups all-purpose flour	1 egg
2 teaspoons baking powder	1 cup sourdough starter
1/4 teaspoon baking soda	1 cup milk
1/2 teaspoon salt	3 tablespoons vegetable oil
1 tablespoon sugar	

In a large bowl, stir together flour, baking powder, baking soda, salt and sugar; set aside. In a medium bowl, beat egg. Stir in sourdough starter, milk and oil. Stir into flour mixture until dry ingredients are just moistened. Preheat griddle according to manufacturer's directions. Or place griddle over medium-high heat until a drop of water bounces across surface. Grease griddle. For each pancake, pour 1/4 to 1/2 cup batter onto preheated griddle. Cook 1 to 2 minutes on each side or until golden brown. Makes 4 to 6 servings.

Variations

Pecan Pancakes: Gently fold 3/4 to 1 cup chopped pecans into batter. Serve with Apricot Syrup, page 111.

Blueberry Pancakes: Gently fold 1 cup fresh, frozen or canned blueberries, well-drained, into batter.

Banana Pancakes: Gently fold 3/4 to 1 cup sliced, diced or mashed banana into batter. Serve with Banana Sauce, page 110.

Pineapple Pancakes: Thoroughly drain 3/4 to 1 cup crushed pineapple. Gently stir into batter. Serve with Cinnamon Syrup, page 111.

Bacon Pancakes: Cook 6 to 8 bacon slices until crisp. Crumble and gently fold into batter.

Applesauce Pancakes: Stir 1/2 teaspoon ground cinnamon into 1 cup applesauce. Stir into batter.

Quick Cottage Cheese Pancakes: Gently fold 1 cup creamed cottage cheese into batter.

Orange Sauce

An elegant dessert sauce. Serve over crepes, pancakes or waffles.

1/2 cup butter or margarine, melted	5 tablespoons orange juice
1-1/2 cups powdered sugar	1 tablespoon grated orange peel

In a chafing dish or small saucepan, melt butter or margarine over low heat. Stir in powdered sugar, orange juice and orange peel. Stir occasionally over low heat 3 to 5 minutes or until thoroughly heated. Pour into a pitcher. Serve hot. Makes about 1 cup.

Serving suggestion:
Fold 24 crepes in half. Arrange on a hot platter with folded crepes overlapping. Pour about 3/4 cup hot Orange Sauce over crepes. Garnish with orange slices. Pour remaining sauce into a small pitcher. Saturate 3 or 4 sugar cubes with lemon extract. Arrange soaked sugar cubes on orange slices. Ignite with a long-handled match. Or warm 2 tablespoons of your favorite liqueur. Touch the surface with a lighted match. Carefully pour the flaming liqueur over sauce and crepes. Serve with remaining sauce.

Old-Fashioned Sourdough Pancakes

Just waiting for your favorite topping.

Overnight Starter, see below
2 tablespoons sugar
1 teaspoon salt
1/2 teaspoon baking powder
3 tablespoons shortening, melted, or
   vegetable oil

2 eggs
1/2 teaspoon baking soda
1 tablespoon water

Overnight Starter:
2 cups all-purpose flour
2 cups warm water (105F, 40C)

1/2 cup sourdough starter

Prepare Overnight Starter the night before according to directions below. Next morning, remove 1/2 cup sourdough starter. Pour into a small plastic or glass container with a tight-fitting lid. Store in refrigerator until needed to make other sourdough products. Or add to other starter in refrigerator. In a small bowl, combine sugar, salt and baking powder. Stir into remaining Overnight Starter mixture. Stir in shortening or oil. Add eggs one at a time, beating well after each addition. In a small bowl, combine baking soda and water. Gently fold baking soda mixture into sourdough mixture. Do not stir after baking soda has been added. Preheat griddle according to manufacturer's directions. Or place griddle over medium-high heat until a drop of water bounces across surface. Grease griddle. For each pancake, pour 1/4 to 1/2 cup batter onto preheated griddle. Cook 1 to 2 minutes on each side or until golden brown. Makes 4 to 6 servings.

Overnight Starter:
In a large bowl, combine all ingredients. Cover with waxed paper or a cloth. Set in a warm place free from drafts. Let stand overnight or 24 hours.

Onion Pancakes

Make these to serve with your favorite creamed vegetable, ham or tuna.

1/3 cup finely chopped onion
1 tablespoon butter or margarine
1-1/4 cups all-purpose flour
2 teaspoons baking powder
1/4 teaspoon baking soda
1/2 teaspoon salt

1 tablespoon sugar
1 egg
1 cup sourdough starter
1 cup milk
2 tablespoons vegetable oil

In a small skillet, sauté onion in butter or margarine over low heat until tender; set aside. In a large bowl, stir together flour, baking powder, baking soda, salt and sugar; set aside. In a medium bowl, beat egg. Stir in sourdough starter, milk and oil. Stir into flour mixture until dry ingredients are just moistened. Fold in sautéed onions. Preheat griddle according to manufacturer's directions. Or place griddle over medium-high heat until a drop of water bounces across surface. Grease griddle. For each pancake, pour 1/4 to 1/2 cup batter onto preheated griddle. Cook 1 to 2 minutes on each side or until golden brown. Serve hot. Makes 4 to 6 servings.

How to Cook Sourdough Pancakes

1/Preheat and grease griddle. For each pancake, pour 1/4 to 1/2 cup batter onto preheated griddle.

2/Cook 1 to 2 minutes on each side or until lightly browned. Turn pancakes when outer edge dries slightly.

Orange Pancakes

A real eye-opener for any morning!

1 cup all-purpose flour
1 teaspoon baking powder
1/2 teaspoon baking soda
1/2 teaspoon salt
2 tablespoons sugar
2 eggs

1 cup sourdough starter
1 cup orange juice
3 tablespoons butter or margarine, melted,
   or vegetable oil
Orange Syrup, page 111, warmed

In a large bowl, stir together flour, baking powder, baking soda, salt and sugar; set aside. In a medium bowl, beat eggs. Stir in sourdough starter, orange juice and butter, margarine or oil. Stir into flour mixture until dry ingredients are just moistened. Preheat griddle according to manufacturer's directions. Or place griddle over medium-high heat until a drop of water bounces across surface. Grease griddle. For each pancake, pour 1/4 to 1/2 cup batter onto preheated griddle. Cook 1 to 2 minutes on each side or until golden brown. Serve pancakes with warm Orange Syrup. Makes 4 servings.

Basic Sourdough Crepes

Wrap these basic crepes around ham, beef or broccoli. Top with a savory sauce.

3 eggs
2 cups sourdough starter
About 3/4 cup milk
1/4 teaspoon salt

1/8 teaspoon baking soda
3 tablespoons butter or margarine, melted
2 to 3 tablespoons milk for thinner batter,
   if desired

In blender, combine all ingredients, using 3/4 cup milk. Process about 1 minute or until batter is smooth and has consistency of heavy cream. If batter is too thick, add more milk, 1 tablespoon at a time. Batter may be cooked immediately or may be refrigerated several hours before cooking. To cook, preheat crepe pan according to manufacturer's directions. Or heat a medium skillet over medium-high heat until a drop of water bounces over surface. Lightly grease pan or skillet. Pour in 2 to 3 tablespoons batter. Quickly lift and tilt pan or skillet, swirling batter so it covers bottom of pan in a thin layer. Cook crepe 10 to 20 seconds until bottom is lightly browned and top is firm to touch. Carefully turn with a spatula. Cook on other side 5 to 7 seconds or until lightly browned. Repeat with remaining batter. Add grease to pan or skillet if crepes stick. To refrigerate, place squares of waxed paper between cooked crepes. Place in airtight bags or plastic containers. Use within 3 to 4 days. Frozen crepes break easily. To prevent breakage in freezer, place squares of waxed paper between cooked crepes and package in an airtight container with firm sides. Store in freezer up to 4 months. Reheat just before serving. Makes about 30 crepes.

Variations

If using an upside-down crepe griddle, blend 2 tablespoons all-purpose flour into basic batter.

Crepe Suzettes: Add 2 tablespoons sugar, 1 teaspoon grated orange peel or lemon peel and 1/4 teaspoon vanilla extract.

Complete instructions for preparing crepes in a conventional pan or an upside-down crepe pan are in Mable Hoffman's excellent book, *Crepe Cookery.* This book shows how to roll and fold crepes for different styles, gives you 26 additional recipes for batter, and includes 200 delicious recipes to make crepes for every occasion. Published by HPBooks®.

Pancake Supreme, page 106.

Pancake Supreme   Photo on page 105.

Meringue topping adds glamour to these dessert pancakes.

Meringue Mix, see below
1 cup all-purpose flour
2 teaspoons baking powder
1/8 teaspoon baking soda
1/4 teaspoon salt
1 tablespoon sugar
1 egg
1/2 cup sourdough starter
1/4 cup half and half

1 cup milk
2 tablespoons butter or margarine, melted
2 tablespoons butter or margarine, melted
About 1 cup packed brown sugar
1 pt. fresh strawberries, halved,
    sprinkled with sugar, or
    1 (11-oz.) pkg. frozen strawberries,
    thawed

Meringue Mix:
3 egg whites
1/2 cup sugar

2 tablespoons water

Prepare Meringue Mix; set aside. In a medium bowl, stir together flour, baking powder, baking soda, salt and sugar; set aside. In a small bowl, beat egg. Stir in sourdough starter, half and half, milk and 2 tablespoons butter or margarine. Stir into flour mixture until dry ingredients are just moistened. Preheat griddle according to manufacturer's directions. Or place griddle over medium-high heat until a drop of water bounces across surface. Grease griddle. For each pancake, pour about 1/3 cup batter onto preheated griddle. Spread to make 6- to 8-inch pancakes. Bake 1 to 2 minutes on each side or until golden brown. Spread each pancake with melted butter or margarine. Sprinkle each with about 1 tablespoon brown sugar. Stack 6 or more pancakes on an oven-proof platter or on a broiler pan. Cover completely with Meringue Mix. Place under broiler 1 to 2 minutes or until golden on top. Decorate meringue with slices of strawberries. Or pour strawberries into a small saucepan. Stir over medium heat until almost to a boil. Cut stack of pancakes in wedges and serve with hot strawberries. Makes 6 to 8 servings.

Meringue Mix:

In a medium bowl, beat egg whites with electric mixer until stiff peaks form; set aside. In a small saucepan, combine sugar and water. Stir constantly over medium-high heat until sugar dissolves and mixture begins to simmer. Beating constantly with electric mixer, pour syrup into stiffly beaten egg whites until mixture stands in peaks.

Buckwheat Pancakes

An old-time favorite.

1 cup sourdough starter
About 1/2 cup milk
1 tablespoon vegetable oil
1 egg, beaten

1 cup buckwheat pancake mix
2 tablespoons milk for thinner batter,
    if desired

In a medium bowl, combine sourdough starter, 1/2 cup milk, oil and egg. Stir in pancake mix. If batter is too thick, add more milk, 1 tablespoon at a time. Preheat griddle according to manufacturer's directions. Or place griddle over medium-high heat until a drop of water bounces across surface. Grease griddle. For each pancake, pour 1/4 to 1/2 cup batter onto preheated griddle. Cook 1 to 2 minutes on each side or until golden brown. Makes 4 to 6 servings.

How to Make Pancake Supreme

1/Spread each pancake with melted butter or margarine. Sprinkle each with about 1 tablespoon brown sugar.

2/Stack 6 pancakes on an oven-proof platter or broiler pan. Cover completely with Meringue Mix. Brown in boiler.

Cornmeal Pancakes

Top these main-dish pancakes with Chicken a la King, page 152, or creamed vegetables.

1/2 cup cornmeal	1 egg
1/2 cup all-purpose flour	1/2 cup sourdough starter
1 teaspoon baking powder	1/2 cup milk
1/2 teaspoon baking soda	1/3 cup dairy sour cream
1/2 teaspoon salt	1-1/2 tablespoons shortening, melted, or
2 teaspoons sugar	vegetable oil

In a medium bowl, stir together cornmeal, flour, baking powder, baking soda, salt and sugar; set aside. In a small bowl, beat egg. Stir in sourdough starter and milk. Stir into flour mixture until dry ingredients are just moistened. Fold in sour cream and shortening or oil. Preheat griddle according to manufacturer's directions. Or place griddle over medium-high heat until a drop of water bounces across surface. Grease griddle. For each pancake, pour 1/4 to 1/2 cup batter onto preheated griddle. Cook 1 to 2 minutes on each side or until golden brown. Makes 4 to 6 servings.

tip

Serve pancakes with warm syrup and the pancakes will stay warm as they are eaten.

Basic Sourdough Waffles

As good as they look in the picture!

1-1/4 cups all-purpose flour	1 egg
2 teaspoons baking powder	1 cup sourdough starter
1/4 teaspoon baking soda	1/4 cup vegetable oil
1/2 teaspoon salt	3/4 cup milk
1 tablespoon sugar	

In a large bowl, stir together flour, baking powder, baking soda, salt and sugar; set aside. In a medium bowl, beat egg. Stir in sourdough starter, oil and milk. Stir into flour mixture until dry ingredients are just moistened. Preheat waffle iron according to manufacturer's directions. For each waffle, pour 1/4 to 1/2 cup batter onto preheated iron. Bake 1 to 2 minutes or until golden brown. Makes about 4 servings.

Variations

Pecan Waffles: Fold in 1 cup finely chopped pecans.

Apricot-Pecan Waffles: Beat 1 teaspoon grated orange peel into sourdough mixture. Fold 1 cup finely chopped pecans into batter. Serve with Apricot Sauce, page 110.

Granola Waffles: Fold in 3/4 to 1 cup Best-Ever Granola, page 157, or other granola.

Gingerbread Waffles

Delicious when served with applesauce and bacon, or whipped cream and sliced bananas.

2 cups all-purpose flour	1 teaspoon ground ginger
2 teaspoons baking powder	2 eggs
1/2 teaspoon baking soda	1/2 cup sourdough starter
1 teaspoon salt	1/2 cup molasses
1/4 cup sugar	6 tablespoons vegetable oil
1/2 teaspoon ground cinnamon	1 cup milk

In a large bowl, stir together flour, baking powder, baking soda, salt, sugar, cinnamon and ginger; set aside. In a medium bowl, beat eggs. Stir in sourdough starter, molasses, oil and milk. Stir into flour mixture until dry ingredients are just moistened. Preheat waffle iron according to manufacturer's directions. For each waffle, pour 1/4 to 1/2 cup batter onto preheated iron. Bake 1 to 2 minutes or until golden brown. Waffles will be soft when taken from iron but will become firm as they stand. Makes 4 to 6 servings.

tip

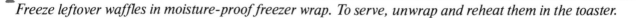

Freeze leftover waffles in moisture-proof freezer wrap. To serve, unwrap and reheat them in the toaster.

Apricot-Pecan Waffles

Banana Sauce

Special for banana fans.

1 large banana, crushed
1 tablespoon lemon juice
2 tablespoons whipping cream or
   evaporated milk

2 cups powdered sugar

In a medium bowl, combine crushed banana and lemon juice. Add cream or evaporated milk. Beat with electric mixer until blended. Add powdered sugar and beat until blended. Spoon into a small serving bowl. Makes about 1 cup.

Apricot Sauce

Serve this sauce with Apricot-Pecan Waffles, page 108.

1 (8-3/4-oz.) can unpeeled apricot halves
1/2 cup light corn syrup
1 tablespoon lemon juice

3 tablespoons honey or 5 tablespoons sugar
2 tablespoons cornstarch
1 cup apricot nectar

Drain apricot halves, reserving juice. Slice fruit and set aside. In a medium saucepan, blend reserved apricot juice, corn syrup, lemon juice and honey or sugar; set aside. In a small bowl, combine cornstarch and 1/4 cup apricot nectar. Stir until smooth. Stir cornstarch mixture and remaining apricot nectar into corn syrup mixture. Cook and stir over medium heat until mixture thickens and bubbles. Stir in cut apricots. Pour into a pitcher. Serve warm. Makes about 2 cups.

Brandy Sauce

A small amount of brandy makes this sauce special.

3/4 cup water
2 cups powdered sugar

1/2 cup butter or margarine
1 tablespoon brandy or brandy flavoring

In a medium saucepan, combine water and powdered sugar. Bring to a boil over medium heat. Stirring occasionally, boil 5 minutes. Remove from heat. Stir in butter or margarine until melted. Stir in brandy or brandy flavoring. Pour into a pitcher. Serve hot. Makes about 1-1/2 cups.

Serving suggestion:
Fold 24 crepes in half. Arrange on a hot platter with folded crepes overlapping. Pour about 3/4 cup hot Brandy Sauce over folded crepes. Pour remaining sauce into a small pitcher. Serve with remaining sauce.

Rum Sauce

For those who love that good rum taste.

1 cup sugar
1/2 cup water
5 tablespoons butter or margarine
1 teaspoon grated orange peel

2 tablespoons orange juice
1/4 cup rum or 1 to 2 teaspoons
   imitation rum extract

In a medium saucepan, combine sugar and water. Bring to a boil over medium heat. Stirring occasionally, boil 5 minutes. Stir in butter or margarine until melted. Stir in orange peel, orange juice and rum or rum extract. Pour into a pitcher. Serve hot. Makes about 1-1/2 cups.

Orange Syrup

Excellent served with Orange Pancakes, page 103.

1 cup sugar
2 tablespoons cornstarch

1 cup orange juice
1/4 cup butter or margarine

In a small saucepan, combine sugar and cornstarch. Slowly stir in orange juice. Add butter or margarine. Stirring constantly, bring to a boil over medium heat. Cook and stir until slightly thickened. Pour into a pitcher. Serve hot or cold. Makes about 1-1/2 cups.

Cinnamon Syrup

Make ahead of time and reheat for serving.

3/4 cup packed brown sugar
1/4 teaspoon ground cinnamon
1/4 cup butter or margarine

1/4 cup water
3 tablespoons light corn syrup

In a small saucepan, combine all ingredients. Cook and stir over medium heat 10 to 15 minutes or until sugar dissolves and mixture thickens slightly. Pour into a pitcher. Serve hot. Makes about 1 cup.

Apricot Syrup

A dessert syrup to complement any waffle, crepe or pancake.

1-1/2 tablespoons cornstarch
2 tablespoons sugar
1 cup apricot nectar

1/4 cup apricot marmalade
1/2 cup light corn syrup
1 tablespoon butter or margarine

In a small saucepan, combine cornstarch and sugar. Slowly stir in apricot nectar until mixture is smooth. Add marmalade, corn syrup and butter or margarine. Stirring constantly, bring to a boil over medium heat. Cook and stir about 10 minutes or until slightly thickened. Pour into a pitcher. Serve hot or cold. Makes about 1-1/2 cups.

Cookies & Brownies

This is probably the most surprising part of sourdough cookery—even to experienced sourdough cooks. You may wonder how the tangy flavor of sourdough will blend with spices, fruits and nuts. It is delicious.

These cookies present a variety of doughs, interesting shapes and intriguing flavors. They include drop cookies, molded cookies, hard and soft cookies, brownies and gooey but delightful surprises. You'll also discover new techniques for working with sourdough. Whether you bake cookies that are dropped from a spoon, shaped or decorated, keeping the cookie jar filled with cookies made from sourdough will be fun and exciting.

In addition to Chocolate Cake Brownies, made with unsweetened cocoa powder, you'll enjoy Peanut Butter Brownies, made with peanut butter and chocolate. The topping is chocolate frosting mixed with peanut butter and nuts. Applesauce Brownies are flavored with applesauce, cinnamon and nutmeg. When cooled, they are drizzled with a sweet cinnamon-applesauce topping. Have you ever tasted a brownie made with potatoes? You'll be delighted with Potato Brownies. They are rich and moist. Frost with your favorite icing or sprinkled them with powdered sugar.

Crushed candy gives Stained-Glass Cookies their glassy appearance. If you prefer not to have the stained-glass centers, just make the outlines with the delicious dough. The baked dough will hold its shape and make attractive open decorations. Paint the dough with Egg-Yolk Paint from the Sugar Cookies recipe.

Ann's Crisp Oatmeal Cookies

Crisp and crunchy.

3/4 cup shortening
1/2 cup granulated sugar
1/2 cup packed brown sugar
1 egg
1 teaspoon vanilla extract
1/2 cup sourdough starter

3/4 cup all-purpose flour
1/4 teaspoon baking soda
1/2 teaspoon salt
1-3/4 cups rolled oats
1 cup raisins, if desired

Grease a large baking sheet; set aside. Preheat oven to 375F (190C). In a large bowl, cream shortening, granulated sugar and brown sugar. Beat in egg and vanilla until mixture is fluffy. Stir in sourdough starter; set aside. In a medium bowl, stir together flour, baking soda and salt. Stir into sourdough mixture. Beat with mixer on medium speed until thoroughly blended. Stir in rolled oats and raisins, if desired. Drop by rounded teaspoonfuls 2 inches apart onto prepared baking sheet. Bake in preheated oven 10 to 12 minutes or until golden brown. Remove from baking sheet. Cool on a rack. Clean and grease baking sheet before baking more cookies. Makes 30 to 40 cookies.

Variation

For a crisper, more pebbly cookie, add 1/2 cup all-purpose flour.

Oat-Chip Cookies

Nutritious ingredients children can't resist.

1 cup shortening
1 cup packed brown sugar
1 cup granulated sugar
2 eggs
1 teaspoon vanilla extract
1/2 cup sourdough starter
1/2 cup milk

2 cups all-purpose flour
1/2 teaspoon baking powder
1 teaspoon baking soda
1/2 teaspoon salt
2 cups rolled oats
1 cup chopped pecans
1 (6-oz.) pkg. chocolate pieces

Grease a large baking sheet; set aside. Preheat oven to 350F (175C). In a large bowl, cream shortening, brown sugar and granulated sugar. Beat in eggs and vanilla until mixture is fluffy. Stir in sourdough starter and milk; set aside. In a medium bowl, stir together flour, baking powder, baking soda and salt. Stir into sourdough mixture. Stir in rolled oats, pecans and chocolate pieces. Drop by rounded teaspoonfuls 2 inches apart onto prepared baking sheet. Bake in preheated oven 12 to 15 minutes. Cool about 2 minutes, then remove from baking sheet. Cool on a rack. Clean and grease baking sheet before baking more cookies. Makes about 90 cookies.

Variation

Omit pecans and chocolate pieces. Add 1 cup raisins and 1 cup peanuts.

Soft Oatmeal Cookies

Special for soft-cookie fans.

1 cup shortening
1 cup granulated sugar
1/2 cup packed brown sugar
1 egg
1 teaspoon vanilla extract
1/4 cup water
1 cup sourdough starter

1-1/2 cups all-purpose flour
1/2 teaspoon baking soda
1 teaspoon salt
2-1/2 cups rolled oats
1 cup raisins, if desired
1/2 cup chopped walnuts or pecans,
  if desired

Grease a large baking sheet; set aside. Preheat oven to 400F (205C). In a large bowl, cream shortening, granulated sugar and brown sugar. Beat in egg and vanilla until mixture is fluffy. Stir in water and sourdough starter; set aside. In a medium bowl, stir together flour, baking soda and salt. Stir into sourdough mixture. Stir in rolled oats. Stir in raisins and nuts, if desired. Drop by rounded teaspoonfuls 2 inches apart onto prepared baking sheet. Bake in preheated oven 10 to 12 minutes or until golden brown. Remove from baking sheet. Cool on a rack. Clean and grease baking sheet before baking more cookies. Makes 50 to 60 cookies.

Banana-Oatmeal Cookies

Very ripe bananas give a rich banana flavor.

1 cup shortening
1-1/2 cups sugar
2 eggs
1/2 cup sourdough starter
2 cups all-purpose flour
1/4 teaspoon baking soda
1/2 teaspoon salt

1 teaspoon ground cinnamon
1/4 teaspoon ground nutmeg
1 cup mashed ripe bananas
2 cups rolled oats
1/2 cup chopped walnuts or pecans,
  if desired
1 cup raisins, if desired

Grease a large baking sheet; set aside. Preheat oven to 375F (190C). In a large bowl, cream shortening and sugar. Beat in eggs until mixture is fluffy. Stir in sourdough starter; set aside. In a medium bowl, stir together flour, baking soda, salt, cinnamon and nutmeg. Stir into sourdough mixture. Stir in bananas until blended. Stir in rolled oats. Stir in nuts and raisins, if desired. Drop by rounded teaspoonfuls 2 inches apart onto prepared baking sheet. Dip blade of a table knife or small metal spatula in water and use to flatten dough mounds. Bake in preheated oven 15 minutes or until golden brown. Remove from baking sheet. Cool on a rack. Clean and grease baking sheet before baking more cookies. Makes 60 to 70 cookies.

Pumpkin-Spice Cookies

These soft cookies make excellent Halloween treats.

1/4 cup shortening
1/2 cup sugar
1 egg
1/2 cup sourdough starter
1/2 cup canned pumpkin
1 cup all-purpose flour
2 teaspoons baking powder

1/2 teaspoon salt
1-1/2 teaspoons ground cinnamon
1/4 teaspoon ground nutmeg
1/8 teaspoon ground ginger
1/2 cup raisins
1/2 cup chopped walnuts or pecans

Grease a large baking sheet; set aside. Preheat oven to 350F (175C). In a medium bowl, cream shortening and sugar. Beat in egg until mixture is fluffy. Stir in sourdough starter and pumpkin; set aside. In a small bowl, stir together flour, baking powder, salt, cinnamon, nutmeg and ginger. Stir into sourdough mixture until blended. Stir in raisins and nuts. Drop by rounded teaspoonfuls 2 inches apart onto prepared baking sheet. Bake in preheated oven 15 minutes or until lightly browned. Remove from baking sheet. Cool on a rack. Clean and grease baking sheet before baking more cookies. Makes 40 to 50 cookies.

Variation

Use mashed canned yams or mashed canned sweet potatoes in place of pumpkin.

Molasses Cookies

Soft and delicious.

1 egg
1/2 cup vegetable oil
1/4 cup sugar
3/4 cup molasses
1/2 cup sourdough starter
2 cups whole-wheat flour

3 tablespoons nonfat milk powder
1/2 teaspoon salt
1 teaspoon ground ginger
1 teaspoon ground cinnamon
2 tablespoons wheat germ

Grease a large baking sheet; set aside. Preheat oven to 350F (175C). In a large bowl, beat egg. Stir in oil, sugar, molasses and sourdough starter. In a medium bowl, stir together remaining ingredients. Add 1/3 at a time to sourdough mixture, beating well after each addition. Drop dough by rounded teaspoonfuls about 3 inches apart onto prepared baking sheet. Dip blade of a table knife or small metal spatula into hot water. Use to flatten each mound of dough until 1/4 inch thick. Bake in preheated oven 10 to 12 minutes or until lightly browned. Let cool about 3 minutes before removing from baking sheet. Cool on a rack. Clean and grease baking sheet before baking more cookies. Makes 36 to 48 cookies.

Ambrosia Drops

Helps pretty-up a tray of cookies.

1/2 cup butter or margarine
1/2 cup sugar
1 egg
1 tablespoon grated orange peel
1/2 cup sourdough starter
1-1/4 cups all-purpose flour

1/2 teaspoon baking powder
1/2 teaspoon salt
1 cup chopped pecans
1 cup shredded coconut
24 to 36 pecan halves

Grease a large baking sheet; set aside. Preheat oven to 375F (190C). In a large bowl, cream butter or margarine and sugar. Beat in egg and orange peel until mixture is fluffy. Stir in sourdough starter; set aside. In a medium bowl, stir together flour, baking powder and salt. Stir into sourdough mixture. Stir in chopped pecans and coconut. Drop by rounded tablespoonfuls 2 inches apart onto prepared baking sheet. Press a pecan half onto center of each cookie. Bake in preheated oven 12 to 14 minutes or until lightly browned. Remove from baking sheet. Cool on a rack. Clean and grease baking sheet before baking more cookies. Makes 24 to 36 cookies.

Sourdough Drop Cookies

This makes a thin, lacy-edged cookie. For a traditional drop cookie, follow the variation.

1/2 cup sourdough starter
1 cup evaporated milk
2 cups all-purpose flour
1/2 teaspoon baking soda
1/2 teaspoon salt
1 cup butter or margarine
1-1/4 cups packed dark brown sugar

1 egg
1 teaspoon vanilla extract
3 cups crushed cornflakes
3/4 cup chopped walnuts or pecans
3/4 cup shredded coconut
1 cup raisins, if desired

In a medium bowl, combine sourdough starter, evaporated milk and 1-1/2 cups flour. Let stand 2 hours at room temperature. In a small bowl, stir together remaining 1/2 cup flour, baking soda and salt; set aside. Grease a large baking sheet; set aside. Preheat oven to 375F (190C). In a large bowl, cream butter or margarine and brown sugar. Beat in egg and vanilla until mixture is fluffy. Stir in flour mixture containing baking soda. Stir in sourdough mixture until blended. Stir in cornflakes, nuts, coconut and raisins, if desired. Drop by rounded teaspoonfuls 2 inches apart onto prepared baking sheet. Bake in preheated oven 15 minutes. Remove from baking sheet. Cool on a rack. Clean and grease baking sheet before baking more cookies. Makes about 60 cookies.

Variation

To mix and bake immediately, cream butter or margarine and sugar. Beat in egg and vanilla until mixture is fluffy. Stir in sourdough starter and milk; set aside. Combine flour, baking soda and salt. Stir into sourdough mixture. Stir in cornflakes, nuts, coconut and raisins, if desired. Bake as directed above.

Sugar Cookies, page 120.

Pineapple Cookies

Polynesian delight.

1/2 cup shortening
1/2 cup granulated sugar
1/2 cup packed brown sugar
1 egg
1 teaspoon vanilla extract
1/2 cup sourdough starter

1 cup crushed pineapple with juice
2-1/4 cups all-purpose flour
1 teaspoon baking soda
1/4 teaspoon salt
1 cup chopped walnuts or pecans
1 cup shredded coconut

Grease a large baking sheet; set aside. Preheat oven to 350F (175C). In a large bowl, cream shortening, granulated sugar and brown sugar. Beat in egg and vanilla until mixture is fluffy. Stir in sourdough starter and crushed pineapple with juice; set aside. In a medium bowl, stir together flour, baking soda and salt. Stir into sourdough mixture. Stir in nuts and coconut. Drop by rounded teaspoonfuls 2 inches apart onto prepared baking sheet. Bake in preheated oven 12 to 15 minutes or until lightly browned. Do not overbake. Remove from baking sheet. Cool on a rack. Clean and grease baking sheet before baking more cookies. Makes about 48 cookies.

Pineapple-Raisin Cookies

Makes great school-lunch goodies.

1/2 cup butter or margarine
1 cup packed brown sugar
1 egg
1 teaspoon vanilla extract
1/2 cup sourdough starter
1 cup raisins

3/4 cup crushed pineapple with juice
2 cups all-purpose flour
1 teaspoon baking powder
1/2 teaspoon baking soda
1/2 teaspoon salt
3/4 cup chopped walnuts or pecans

Grease a large baking sheet; set aside. Preheat oven to 375F (190C). In a large bowl, cream butter or margarine and brown sugar. Beat in egg and vanilla until mixture is fluffy. Stir in sourdough starter, raisins and pineapple with juice; set aside. In a medium bowl, stir together flour, baking powder, baking soda and salt. Stir into sourdough mixture until blended. Stir in nuts. Drop by rounded teaspoonfuls 2 inches apart onto prepared baking sheet. Bake in preheated oven 12 to 15 minutes or until golden brown. Remove from baking sheet. Cool on a rack. Clean and grease baking sheet before baking more cookies. Makes 50 to 60 cookies.

tip

If you bake 2 trays of cookies at a time, place 1 in the middle of the oven and the other under it. Reverse their positions halfway through baking time.

Fruit Cocktail Cookies

Soft and fruity.

1 cup shortening	4 cups all-purpose flour
1-1/2 cups packed brown sugar	1 teaspoon baking soda
1 egg	1 teaspoon salt
1 teaspoon vanilla extract	1 teaspoon ground cinnamon
1/2 cup sourdough starter	1 teaspoon ground cloves
1 (16-oz.) can fruit cocktail, undrained	1 cup chopped walnuts or pecans

Grease a large baking sheet; set aside. Preheat oven to 375F (190C). In a large bowl, cream shortening and brown sugar. Beat in egg and vanilla until mixture is fluffy. Stir in sourdough starter. Fold in fruit cocktail with juice; set aside. In a medium bowl, stir together flour, baking soda, salt, cinnamon and cloves. Stir into sourdough mixture until dry ingredients are just moistened. Fold in nuts. Drop by rounded teaspoonfuls 2 inches apart onto prepared baking sheet. Bake in preheated oven 15 to 18 minutes or until lightly browned. Remove from baking sheet. Cool on a rack. Clean and grease baking sheet before baking more cookies. Makes 85 to 90 cookies.

Applesauce-Date Drops

Spicy and filled with dates and nuts.

1/2 cup shortening	1 teaspoon salt
1 cup sugar	1 teaspoon ground cinnamon
1 egg	1/4 teaspoon ground cloves
1/2 cup sourdough starter	1 cup unsweetened applesauce
2-1/2 cups all-purpose flour	1 cup finely chopped pitted dates
1/2 teaspoon baking soda	1 cup chopped walnuts or pecans

Grease a large baking sheet; set aside. Preheat oven to 350F (175C). In a large bowl, cream shortening and sugar. Beat in egg until mixture is fluffy. Stir in sourdough starter; set aside. In a medium bowl, stir together flour, baking soda, salt, cinnamon and cloves. Alternately add dry ingredients and applesauce to sourdough mixture. Fold in dates and nuts. Drop by rounded teaspoonfuls 2 inches apart onto prepared baking sheet. Bake in preheated oven 15 to 18 minutes or until lightly browned. Remove from baking sheet. Cool on a rack. Clean and grease baking sheet before baking more cookies. Makes 50 to 60 cookies.

Sugar Cookies   Photo on page 117.

Egg-yolk paint adds colorful details to these rolled cookies.

1 cup shortening	4-1/2 cups all-purpose flour
1-1/2 cups sugar	1/2 teaspoon baking soda
3 eggs	1 teaspoon salt
1-1/2 teaspoons lemon or almond extract	Egg-Yolk Paint, see below
1 teaspoon vanilla extract	Icing, if desired, see below
1/2 cup sourdough starter	

Egg-Yolk Paint:

3 or 4 egg yolks	1 tablespoon white corn syrup
5 teaspoons water	Food coloring

Icing:

3 egg whites, room temperature	1/2 teaspoon cream of tartar
1 (1-lb.) box powdered sugar	

In a large bowl, cream shortening and sugar. Beat in eggs, lemon or almond extract and vanilla until mixture is fluffy. Stir in sourdough starter; set aside. In a medium bowl, stir together flour, baking soda and salt. Stir into sourdough mixture. Refrigerate dough 1 hour. Preheat oven to 350F (175C). Roll out dough 1/4 inch thick and cut into desired shapes. Arrange on an ungreased baking sheet. Bake in preheated oven 10 to 12 minutes or until very lightly browned. Remove from baking sheet. Cool on a rack. Clean baking sheet before baking more cookies. Prepare Egg-Yolk Paint. Prepare Icing, if desired. Use a small paint brush to paint cooled cookies with Egg-Yolk Paint. If desired, decorate with Icing. Makes 48 to 60 cookies.

Egg-Yolk Paint:

In a small bowl, blend egg yolks, water, corn syrup and desired food coloring. If more than one color is made, divide mixture into small jars before adding coloring.

Icing:

In a medium bowl, combine ingredients. Beat with electric mixer on high speed 7 to 10 minutes. Keep bowl covered with a damp cloth to prevent drying. Spoon into a decorator tube. Use a small tip. Icing becomes very hard when dry.

tip

Leave space between cookies on the baking sheet. Crowding causes cookies to cook unevenly and may cause uneven browning.

How to Make Sugar Cookies

1/Divide egg-yolk paint into small bowls before adding coloring. Use a small clean brush to paint cookies.

2/Raised outlines are made with icing pressed from a pastry tube or parchment cone.

Butteroons

Delicate fruit flavored cookie coated with coconut.

1/2 cup butter	1/4 teaspoon salt
1/2 cup sugar	1/2 cup sourdough starter
1 egg	2/3 cup well-drained crushed pineapple
2 teaspoons grated lemon peel	1-1/2 cups all-purpose flour
2 teaspoons grated orange peel	2 cups shredded coconut

Preheat oven to 325F (165C). In a large bowl, cream butter and sugar. Beat in egg, lemon peel, orange peel and salt until mixture is fluffy. Stir in sourdough starter and drained pineapple. Stir in flour. Pour 1 cup coconut into a 9-inch pie plate. Drop dough by rounded teaspoonfuls onto coconut. Roll until cookie mixture is coated with coconut. Add more coconut as needed. Arrange coated balls 1 inch apart on an ungreased baking sheet. Bake in preheated oven 10 to 15 minutes or until lightly browned. Remove from baking sheet. Cool on a rack. Clean baking sheet before baking more cookies. Makes 24 to 36 cookies.

Peanut Blossoms

Chocolate kisses make tasty centers for these blossoms.

1/2 cup peanut butter
1/2 cup butter or margarine
1/2 cup granulated sugar
1/2 cup packed brown sugar
1 egg
1 teaspoon vanilla extract
1/2 cup sourdough starter

2 cups all-purpose flour
1/2 teaspoon baking powder
1/2 teaspoon baking soda
1/2 teaspoon salt
1/4 to 1/3 cup granulated sugar
36 chocolate kisses

Preheat oven to 375F (190C). In a large bowl, cream peanut butter, butter or margarine, granulated sugar and brown sugar. Beat in egg and vanilla until mixture is fluffy. Stir in sourdough starter; set aside. In a medium bowl, stir together flour, baking powder, baking soda and salt. Stir into sourdough mixture. Refrigerate 1 hour. Shape into 1-inch balls and roll in granulated sugar. Arrange 2 inches apart on a large ungreased baking sheet. Bake in preheated oven 8 minutes. Cookies will be soft. Press candy kisses flat side down into center of each cookie. Return to oven and bake 2 to 5 minutes. Remove from baking sheet. Cool on a rack. Clean baking sheet before baking more cookies. Makes about 36 cookies.

Chocolate & Peanut Cookies

Young people make these disappear in a hurry.

1/2 cup shortening
1/2 cup butter or margarine
1-1/2 cups packed brown sugar
2 eggs
2 teaspoons vanilla extract
1 cup sourdough starter

3-1/2 cups all-purpose flour
1/2 teaspoon baking soda
1 teaspoon salt
2 cups salted peanuts
1 (6-oz.) pkg. semisweet chocolate pieces
Granulated sugar

Lightly grease a large baking sheet; set aside. Preheat oven to 375F (190C). In a large bowl, cream shortening, butter or margarine and brown sugar. Beat in eggs and vanilla until mixture is fluffy. Stir in sourdough starter; set aside. In a medium bowl, stir together flour, baking soda and salt. Stir into sourdough mixture. Stir in peanuts and chocolate pieces. Drop dough by rounded teaspoonfuls 2 inches apart onto prepared baking sheet. Grease bottom of a drinking glass. Dip in granulated sugar. Flatten each mound of dough with bottom of glass. Dip bottom of glass in granulated sugar as needed. Bake in preheated oven 15 to 20 minutes or until golden brown. Immediately remove cookies from baking sheet. Cool on a rack. Clean and grease baking sheet before baking more cookies. Makes 60 to 70 cookies.

Chocolate Balls   Photo on cover.

Stored in a pretty container—the perfect gift for the person with a sweet tooth.

1 cup sourdough starter
1-3/4 cups granulated sugar
1/2 cup vegetable oil
2 teaspoons vanilla extract
4 (1-oz.) squares semisweet chocolate,
  melted
3 eggs

1/4 cup nonfat milk powder
3-1/2 cups all-purpose flour
1/4 teaspoon baking soda
1/4 teaspoon salt
1 cup chopped walnuts or pecans
1-1/2 to 2 cups powdered sugar

In a large bowl, combine sourdough starter, granulated sugar, oil, vanilla, melted chocolate, eggs and milk powder. Beat with electric mixer on medium speed until smooth; set aside. In a medium bowl, stir together flour, baking soda and salt. Stir into sourdough mixture. Stir in nuts. Place in freezer 1 to 2 hours or in refrigerator overnight. Grease a large baking sheet; set aside. Preheat oven to 375F (190C). If dough has been held in freezer 2 hours, use about 1 tablespoon dough for each cookie. Shape into balls and roll in powdered sugar. Arrange 2 inches apart on prepared baking sheet. If dough has been refrigerated overnight, drop by rounded teaspoonfuls 2 inches apart on prepared baking sheet. Sprinkle lightly with powdered sugar. Bake in preheated oven 10 to 12 minutes. Remove from baking sheet. Cool on a rack. Clean and grease baking sheet before baking more cookies. Makes 70 to 90 cookies.

Choco-Orange Chippers

You'll love these soft and not-too-sweet cookies.

1/2 cup butter or margarine
1 (3-oz.) pkg. cream cheese,
  room temperature
1/4 cup packed brown sugar
1/4 cup granulated sugar
1 egg
1 teaspoon grated orange peel
1/2 teaspoon vanilla extract

1/2 cup sourdough starter
2 cups all-purpose flour
1/2 teaspoon baking soda
1/2 teaspoon salt
1 (6-oz.) pkg. semisweet chocolate pieces
1/2 cup chopped pecans
1/2 cup shredded coconut, if desired

Preheat oven to 375F (190C). In a large bowl, cream butter or margarine, cream cheese, brown sugar and granulated sugar. Beat in egg, orange peel and vanilla until mixture is fluffy. Stir in sourdough starter; set aside. In a medium bowl, stir together flour, baking soda and salt. Stir into sourdough mixture. Stir in chocolate pieces, nuts and coconut, if desired. Drop by rounded teaspoonfuls onto an ungreased baking sheet. Bake in preheated oven 12 to 15 minutes or until golden brown. Remove from baking sheet. Cool on a rack. Clean baking sheet before baking more cookies. Makes 36 to 48 cookies.

Stained-Glass Cookies

Good to eat—and a beautiful way to decorate your Christmas tree. They also make nice gifts.

5 eggs
1/2 cup sourdough starter
1 teaspoon vanilla extract
3-1/2 cups powdered sugar

6-1/2 to 7 cups all-purpose flour
25 to 30 pkgs. Lifesavers or
    about 100 Brach's colored candy balls
1 egg white, slightly beaten

In a large bowl, beat eggs slightly. Stir in sourdough starter, vanilla and powdered sugar. Gradually add enough flour to make a thick dough. Turn out onto a lightly floured surface. Knead 2 or 3 minutes or until smooth. Refrigerate 3 to 4 hours. Cover a large baking sheet with foil. Trace outlines of bells, trees, birds, stars or other pictures on foil. Grease foil or use non-stick spray; set aside. If cookies are to be used as ornaments, cut 50 to 60 pieces of thin string, each 6 inches long; set aside. Separate candies into matching colors. Crush each color separately; set aside. Preheat oven to 350F (175C). Roll chilled dough between your hands into thin ropes the size of a pencil. Lay strands of dough on outlines traced on foil. Pinch end together. Loop pieces of string around top of ornament, if desired. Brush shaped dough with beaten egg white. Spoon crushed candies into centers of cookies as pictured. Bake in preheated oven 5 to 8 minutes or until dough begins to harden. Do not brown. Cool to room temperature before removing from foil. Remove from baking sheet. Cool on a rack. Makes 50 to 60 cookies.

Orange Candy Cookies

Diced orange-slice candy gives an interesting taste and texture to these flavorful cookies.

1 (11-oz.) pkg. orange-slice candy
1/2 cup all-purpose flour
1/2 cup shortening
1-1/2 cups packed brown sugar
2 eggs
1/2 cup sourdough starter
2 cups all-purpose flour

1 teaspoon baking powder
1 teaspoon baking soda
1/2 teaspoon salt
1/2 cup rolled oats
1/2 cup chopped walnuts or pecans
1/2 cup finely shredded coconut

Use a sharp knife to dice candy. Dip blade of knife in water as needed to control stickiness. In a small bowl, combine diced candy and 1/2 cup flour; set aside. Grease a large baking sheet; set aside. Preheat oven to 325F (165C). In a large bowl, cream shortening and brown sugar. Beat in eggs until mixture is fluffy. Stir in sourdough starter; set aside. In a medium bowl, stir together 2 cups flour, baking powder, baking soda and salt. Stir into sourdough mixture. Stir in diced candy mixture and rolled oats. Stir in nuts and coconut. Refrigerate dough 2 hours or overnight. Roll chilled dough into 1-inch balls and arrange on prepared baking sheet. Press down with tines of a fork. Bake 15 to 20 minutes or until lightly browned. Remove from baking sheet. Cool on a rack. Clean and grease baking sheet before baking more cookies. Makes 50 to 60 cookies.

How to Make Stained-Glass Cookies

1/Cover a large baking sheet with foil. Trace outlines of bells, stars or other shapes on foil. Grease foil lightly.

2/Using strands of dough, outline cookie shapes following tracings on foil. Brush with beaten egg white.

3/Separate candies into matching colors. Crush each color separately. Spoon crushed candies into centers of cookies.

Goo-Goo Cookies

Messy to eat, but oh, so good!

1/2 cup shortening	2 cups all-purpose flour
1 cup sugar	1/2 teaspoon baking soda
1 egg	1/2 teaspoon salt
1 teaspoon vanilla extract	20 to 25 marshmallows, cut in half
1/2 cup unsweetened cocoa powder	Chocolate Frosting, see below
1/2 cup sourdough starter	1 cup chopped walnuts or pecans
1/2 cup milk	

Goo-Goo Chocolate Frosting:

1 (1-lb.) box powdered sugar	1 teaspoon vanilla extract
1/2 cup unsweetened cocoa powder	7 tablespoons boiling water
1/4 teaspoon salt	6 tablespoons butter or margarine, softened

Preheat oven to 375F (190C). In a large bowl, cream shortening and sugar. Beat in egg, vanilla and cocoa powder until blended. Stir in sourdough starter and milk; set aside. In a medium bowl, stir together flour, baking soda and salt. Stir into sourdough mixture until smooth. Drop by rounded teaspoonfuls on an ungreased baking sheet. Bake in preheated oven 8 to 10 minutes. Place a marshmallow half, cut side down, on top of each hot cookie. Bake about 1 minute or until marshmallows are puffed but not browned. Remove from baking sheet. Cool on a rack. Clean and grease baking sheet before baking more cookies. Prepare Goo-Goo Chocolate Frosting. Frost cookies, completely covering marshmallows. Decorate each cookie with a sprinkle of chopped nuts. Makes 40 to 50 cookies.

Goo-Goo Chocolate Frosting:
In a medium bowl, combine powdered sugar, cocoa powder and salt. Stir in vanilla and boiling water. Add butter or margarine. Beat until smooth. Frosting thickens as it cools. If it becomes too thick, stir in a few drops hot water.

Carob Cookies

Cinnamon, molasses and sourdough flavor blend to make these a favorite drop cookie.

1/2 cup butter or margarine	2 tablespoons wheat germ
3/4 cup sugar	1 teaspoon baking powder
1 egg	1/2 teaspoon baking soda
2 tablespoons molasses	1/4 cup unsweetened carob powder
1/2 cup sourdough starter	1/4 teaspoon ground cinnamon
1-1/2 cups whole-wheat flour	

Grease a large baking sheet; set aside. Preheat oven to 350F (175C). In a medium bowl, cream butter or margarine and sugar. Beat in egg until mixture is fluffy. Stir in molasses and sourdough starter. In another medium bowl, stir together flour, wheat germ, baking powder, baking soda, carob powder and cinnamon. Add 1/3 at a time to starter mixture, beating well after each addition. Drop by rounded teaspoonfuls onto prepared baking sheet. Bake in preheated oven 8 to 10 minutes. Remove from baking sheet. Cool on a rack. Clean and grease baking sheet before baking more cookies. Makes 36 to 48 cookies.

Jelly Gems

Your favorite jam adds a special flavor to these refrigerator cookies.

1/2 cup butter or margarine
1/4 cup packed brown sugar
1/4 cup granulated sugar
1 egg

1/2 teaspoon vanilla extract
1/2 cup sourdough starter
2 cups all-purpose flour
1/2 (8-oz.) jar jam or jelly

In a large bowl, cream butter or margarine, brown sugar and granulated sugar. Beat in egg and vanilla until mixture is fluffy. Stir in sourdough starter and flour. Flour your hands and shape dough into a roll. Wrap in waxed paper or plastic wrap. Refrigerate 2 hours or overnight. Grease a large baking sheet; set aside. Preheat oven to 400F (205C). Cut chilled dough into 1/4-inch slices. Refrigerate unsliced dough. Arrange slices 2 inches apart on prepared baking sheet. Press your thumb into center of each slice. Spoon 1/2 teaspoon jam or jelly into indentation. Bake in preheated oven 8 to 10 minutes. Remove from baking sheet. Cool on a rack. Clean and grease baking sheet before baking more cookies. Makes 36 to 48 cookies.

Applesauce Brownies

Apples and spice and everything nice.

1/2 cup shortening
1-1/4 cups sugar
2 eggs
1 teaspoon vanilla extract
1/2 cup sourdough starter
2/3 cup applesauce
1/4 cup milk

1 cup all-purpose flour
1 teaspoon baking powder
1/2 teaspoon salt
1 teaspoon ground cinnamon
1/4 teaspoon ground nutmeg
1/2 cup chopped walnuts or pecans
Cinnamon Topping, see below

Cinnamon Topping:
3/4 cup sifted powdered sugar
1/8 teaspoon ground cinnamon

1/4 cup applesauce
1 to 3 teaspoons milk

Grease a 13" x 9" baking pan; set aside. Preheat oven to 350F (175C). In a large bowl, cream shortening and sugar. Beat in eggs and vanilla. Stir in sourdough starter, applesauce and milk; set aside. In a small bowl, stir together flour, baking powder, salt, cinnamon and nutmeg. Stir into sourdough mixture. Stir in nuts. Spread in prepared pan. Bake in preheated oven 40 to 50 minutes or until surface springs back when touched with your fingers. Turn out of pan. Prepare Cinnamon Topping. Drizzle over slightly warm brownies. Cool before slicing. Makes about 24 brownies.

Cinnamon Topping:
In a small bowl, combine powdered sugar, cinnamon and applesauce. Stir in enough milk to make a mixture that will pour from a spoon.

Ann's Fudge Brownies

This is everything a fudge brownie should be!

1/3 cup butter or margarine	1 cup sugar
2 (1-oz.) squares semisweet chocolate	1 egg, beaten
3/4 cup all-purpose flour	1/2 cup sourdough starter
1/2 teaspoon baking soda	1 teaspoon vanilla extract
1/2 teaspoon salt	1/2 cup chopped walnuts or pecans

Grease a 9-inch square baking pan; set aside. Preheat oven to 375F (190C). In a small saucepan, melt butter or margarine and chocolate over low heat; set aside to cool. In a medium bowl, stir together flour, baking soda, salt and sugar; set aside. Stir egg, sourdough starter and vanilla into cooled chocolate mixture. Beat until blended. Stir into flour mixture until blended. Fold in nuts. Spread in prepared pan. For a more even surface after baking, make batter higher in center of pan than on sides. Bake in preheated oven 30 to 35 minutes or until edge begins to pull away from pan. Cut and remove from pan. Makes 12 to 16 servings.

Potato Brownies

Everybody's favorite—made better!

2/3 cup hot water	1/2 cup sourdough starter
1/2 cup instant mashed potatoes	1/2 cup all-purpose flour
1/3 cup shortening	1/2 teaspoon baking powder
2 (1-oz.) squares unsweetened chocolate	1/2 teaspoon salt
1 cup sugar	1/2 cup chopped walnuts or pecans
2 eggs, slightly beaten	

Grease a 9-inch square baking pan or a 12" x 7-1/2" baking pan; set aside. Preheat oven to 350F (175C). In a large bowl, stir hot water into instant potatoes; set aside. In a small saucepan, melt shortening and chocolate over low heat. Stir often. Stir melted chocolate mixture, sugar, eggs and sourdough starter into potato mixture; set aside. In a small bowl, stir together flour, baking powder and salt. Stir into chocolate mixture. Stir in nuts. Pour into prepared pan. Bake in preheated oven 30 minutes or until surface springs back when touched with your fingers. Let stand 5 minutes. Turn out of pan. Cool on a rack before cutting. Makes about 12 servings.

Variation

To frost brownies, sprinkle 1 cup semisweet chocolate pieces over hot brownies. Let stand 3 to 5 minutes until melted, then spread with a spatula.

Blonde Brownies

Be adventurous! These will please any brownie fan.

1/4 cup butter or margarine
1 cup packed brown sugar
1 egg
1/2 teaspoon vanilla extract
1/2 cup sourdough starter

1 cup all-purpose flour
1/2 teaspoon baking soda
1/2 teaspoon salt
1/2 cup coarsely chopped walnuts or pecans
1 (6-oz.) pkg. chocolate pieces

Generously grease an 8-inch square baking pan; set aside. Preheat oven to 350F (175C). In a medium bowl, cream butter or margarine and brown sugar. Beat in egg and vanilla until mixture is fluffy. Stir in sourdough starter; set aside. In a small bowl, stir together flour, baking soda and salt. Stir into sourdough mixture until blended. Stir in nuts. Spread in prepared pan. For a more even surface after baking, make batter higher in center of pan than on sides. Bake in preheated oven 20 to 25 minutes or until surface springs back when touched with your fingers. Do not overbake. Sprinkle chocolate pieces over top of hot brownies. Let stand 5 minutes, then spread to make an icing. Cut while still warm. Makes 12 to 16 servings.

Peanut Butter Brownies

Chocolate and peanut butter combine to make the prefect topping.

1/4 cup shortening
2 (1-oz.) squares unsweetened chocolate
1 cup sugar
1/4 cup peanut butter
1 egg
1/2 cup sourdough starter

1 teaspoon vanilla extract
1/2 cup all-purpose flour
1/2 teaspoon baking soda
1/4 teaspoon salt
Peanut Butter Frosting, see below
1/2 cup chopped walnuts or pecans

Peanut Butter Frosting:
1 (1-lb.) box powdered sugar
1/2 cup unsweetened cocoa powder
1/4 teaspoon salt
1 teaspoon vanilla extract

7 tablespoons boiling water
6 tablespoons butter or margarine, softened
3 tablespoons peanut butter

Grease a 9-inch square baking pan or a 12" x 7-1/2" baking pan; set aside. Preheat oven to 350F (175C). In a small saucepan, melt shortening and chocolate over low heat. Stir often. Stir in sugar and peanut butter until blended. In a medium bowl, beat egg. Stir in sourdough starter, vanilla and chocolate mixture; set aside. In a small bowl, stir together flour, baking soda and salt. Stir into sourdough mixture. Spread in prepared pan. Bake in preheated oven 25 to 30 minutes or until edge begins to pull away from pan. Cool slightly before cutting. Prepare Peanut Butter Frosting. Spread over cooled brownies. Sprinkle with chopped nuts. Cut brownies and remove from pan. Makes 12 to 18 servings.

Peanut Butter Frosting:
In a medium bowl, combine powdered sugar, cocoa powder and salt. Stir in vanilla and boiling water. Add butter or margarine and peanut butter. Beat until smooth. Frosting thickens as it cools. If it becomes too thick, stir in a few drops of hot water.

Sourdough Cakes

Sourdough was used as leavening for cakes long before baking powder was discovered. Used with another leavening agent such as baking powder or baking soda, sourdough starter produces lovely light cakes. The flavor of spices, chocolate, fruits and nuts are even richer than usual when baked in a sourdough batter. You'll be proud to serve the cakes in this section for any occasion. And they're easy, too.

When you serve these special cakes, your family and friends will marvel at the unique sourdough flavor. If a recipe has too much sourdough tang for you, add a pinch of baking soda the next time you make the cake.

Chocolate is a favorite the world over. What could be better than sourdough Chocolate Cake? The recipe in this section makes a rich, moist cake and a thick, velvety Butterscotch-Chocolate Frosting.

Lunch boxes will be opened eagerly when they hold Malted Cupcakes. These tasty cupcakes don't require a frosting—they make their own.

When you plan to entertain and need an elegant dessert, prepare Pumpkin Roll. This lovely filled roll is made like a jelly roll. After it is baked, trim the edges to make it easier to roll. Serve this roll in place of standard pumpkin pie for Thanksgiving, or serve it at a New Year's Eve buffet.

Holiday baking should include cakes heavy with fruit and nuts. Holiday Fruitcakes should be made in the fall and aged in the refrigerator until they are served in December.

Fiesta Cake is similar to a fruitcake. The secret ingredient is mashed pinto beans. They give this cake a moist texture that stays moist. The flavor is even better the second or third day. Butter-Rum Cake has a rich rum-flavored syrup that soaks into the baked cake. You'll be swamped with requests for the recipe after you serve it.

Rincon Spice Cake

As good as a spice cake can be.

1/2 cup shortening
1 cup sugar
2 eggs
1 cup sourdough starter
1 cup milk
1 teaspoon vanilla extract
2 cups all-purpose flour
1 teaspoon baking powder
1/2 teaspoon baking soda

1/2 teaspoon salt
2 teaspoons ground cinnamon
1/2 teaspoon ground nutmeg
1/2 teaspoon ground cloves
1 cup chopped walnuts or pecans, if desired
1/2 cup raisins, if desired
Caramel Icing, see below
1/2 cup chopped walnuts or pecans

Caramel Icing:
1/2 cup butter or margarine
1 cup packed brown sugar
1/4 cup half and half or evaporated milk

About 2-1/2 cups powdered sugar
1 teaspoon vanilla extract

Grease and flour a 13" x 9" baking pan; set aside. Preheat oven to 350F (175C). In a medium bowl, cream shortening and sugar. Add eggs one at a time, beating well after each addition. Stir in sourdough starter, milk and vanilla. Beat with a rotary beater or electric mixer 2 minutes; set aside. In a medium bowl, stir together flour, baking powder, baking soda, salt, cinnamon, nutmeg and cloves. Stir into sourdough mixture. Beat until batter is smooth. Fold in 1 cup nuts and raisins, if desired. Pour into prepared pan. Bake in preheated oven 30 to 40 minutes or until surface springs back when touched with your fingers. Cool cake in pan 5 minutes. Remove from pan. Cool on a rack. Prepare Caramel Icing. Spread over top and sides of cooled cake. Sprinkle 1/2 cup nuts over top of cake. Makes 12 to 18 servings.

Caramel Icing:
Melt butter or margarine in a medium saucepan. Stir in brown sugar. Stir over medium heat until mixture comes to a boil. Reduce heat to low. Stir and boil gently 2 minutes. Stir in half and half or milk, 2 cups powdered sugar and vanilla. Beat with electric mixer until smooth. Add enough of remaining powdered sugar to make a spreading consistency. Makes about 2-1/2 cups.

Fiesta Cake

Not quite a fruitcake, but very special.

1/4 cup butter or margarine	1/2 teaspoon salt
1 cup sugar	1 teaspoon ground cinnamon
1 egg	1/2 teaspoon ground cloves
1 teaspoon vanilla extract	1/2 teaspoon ground allspice
1 cup sourdough starter	1 cup finely diced raw apples
1/2 cup milk	1/2 cup chopped walnuts or pecans
1 cup drained cooked pinto beans, mashed	1 cup raisins
1 cup all-purpose flour	Fiesta Glaze, see below
2 teaspoons baking powder	1/2 cup glacé fruit
1/2 teaspoon baking soda	12 to 15 walnut or pecan halves, if desired

Fiesta Glaze:

1 cup powdered sugar	1 tablespoon butter or margarine, melted
1/4 teaspoon vanilla extract	About 1 tablespoon milk

Generously grease a 12-cup Bundt pan or tube pan; set aside. Preheat oven to 375F (190C). In a large bowl, cream butter or margarine and sugar. Beat in egg and vanilla until mixture is fluffy. Stir in sourdough starter, milk and beans; set aside. In a medium bowl, stir together flour, baking powder, baking soda, salt, cinnamon, cloves and allspice. Beat into sourdough mixture until smooth. Fold in apples, 1/2 cup chopped nuts and raisins. Pour into prepared pan. Bake in preheated oven 50 to 60 minutes or until a wooden pick inserted 2 inches from side comes out clean. Cool in pan 5 minutes. Invert onto a round platter. Remove pan. Cool on a rack. Prepare Fiesta Glaze and pour over cake. Decorate with glacé fruit and walnut or pecan halves, if desired.

Fiesta Glaze:
In a small bowl, combine all ingredients. Beat until smooth.

Choco-Date Cake

Chocolate and dates make an interesting combination.

1 cup boiling water	1-1/2 cups all-purpose flour
1 cup chopped dates	1 teaspoon baking powder
1 cup butter or margarine	3/4 teaspoon baking soda
1 cup granulated sugar	2 tablespoons unsweetened cocoa powder
2 eggs	1 cup semisweet chocolate pieces
1 teaspoon vanilla extract	1/2 cup chopped pecans
1 cup sourdough starter	Powdered sugar, if desired

In a small bowl, pour water over dates; set aside to cool. Grease a 13" x 9" baking pan; set aside. Preheat oven to 350F (175C). In a large bowl, cream butter or margarine and granulated sugar. Beat in eggs and vanilla until fluffy. Stir in cooled date mixture and sourdough starter; set aside. In a medium bowl, stir together flour, baking powder, baking soda and cocoa powder. Stir into sourdough mixture. Fold in chocolate pieces and pecans. Pour into prepared pan. Bake in preheated oven 40 minutes or until surface springs back when touched with your fingers. If desired, sprinkle with powdered sugar. Makes 12 to 18 servings.

Holiday Fruitcakes

Make these cakes in October and serve them in December.

1-1/2 cups butter or margarine
1 cup granulated sugar
1 cup packed brown sugar
6 eggs
1/4 cup milk
1 cup sourdough starter
1 teaspoon lemon extract, if desired
3-1/2 cups all-purpose flour
3 to 4 cups glacé fruit mix

1 to 1-1/2 cups raisins
2 to 3 cups chopped walnuts or pecans
1/2 teaspoon baking soda
1 teaspoon salt
1 teaspoon ground cinnamon
1/2 teaspoon ground nutmeg
1/2 teaspoon ground allspice
1/2 teaspoon ground cloves
1/2 to 1 cup fruit brandy

Grease two 9" x 5" loaf pans or six 5" x 3-1/2" loaf pans. Line with heavy brown paper. Grease paper; set aside. Preheat oven to 300F (150C). In a large bowl, cream butter or margarine, granulated sugar and brown sugar. Beat in eggs one at a time. Stir in milk, sourdough starter and lemon extract, if desired. In a large bowl, stir 1/2 cup flour into fruit mix, raisins and nuts; set aside. In a medium bowl, stir together remaining flour, baking soda, salt, cinnamon, nutmeg, allspice and cloves. Stir into sourdough mixture. Fold in fruit mixture. Pour batter into prepared pans. Bake small loaves about 1-1/2 hours and large loaves about 2-1/2 hours. Or bake until a wooden pick inserted in center of loaf comes out clean. Cool 5 minutes in pan. Turn out of pans. Cool on a rack. When cool, remove paper. **To season:** For each cake soak a cloth in brandy. Wrap cakes in brandy-soaked cloths and wrap airtight in plastic wrap or foil, or place in an airtight plastic container. Store in refrigerator 2 to 3 months to season. Resoak cloths every 3 to 4 weeks. Let cakes season at least 6 to 8 weeks before cutting. Makes 2 large loaves or 6 small loaves.

Gingerbread

Perfect snack for a cold winter's day or night.

1/4 cup butter or margarine
1/2 cup sugar
1 egg
1/2 cup molasses
1 cup sourdough starter
1-1/2 cups all-purpose flour
1 teaspoon baking powder
1/2 teaspoon baking soda

1/2 teaspoon salt
1 teaspoon ground cinnamon
1 teaspoon ground ginger
1/4 teaspoon ground cloves
1/4 teaspoon ground nutmeg
1/2 cup milk
About 1 cup whipped cream, if desired

Grease and flour a 9-inch square baking pan; set aside. Preheat oven to 350F (175C). Cream butter or margarine and sugar. Beat in egg until mixture is fluffy. Stir in molasses and sourdough starter; set aside. In a medium bowl, stir together flour, baking powder, baking soda, salt, cinnamon, ginger, cloves and nutmeg. Beginning and ending with flour mixture, alternately stir flour mixture and milk into sourdough mixture. Beat well after each addition. Scrape bowl often. Turn into prepared pan. Bake in preheated oven 45 to 55 minutes or until surface springs back when touched with your fingers. Serve hot or cold. To serve, cut, remove from pan and arrange on a small platter or on dessert plates. Top each serving with a dollop of whipped cream, if desired. Makes 6 to 9 servings.

Butter-Rum Cake

Rich rum-flavored syrup soaks into the baked cake.

1/3 cup butter	1 cup milk
1/3 cup shortening	2-3/4 cups all-purpose flour
1-3/4 cups sugar	1 tablespoon baking powder
4 eggs	1/2 teaspoon baking soda
1 teaspoon vanilla extract	1 teaspoon salt
1 tablespoon rum extract	Butter-Rum Syrup, see below
3/4 cup sourdough starter	

Butter-Rum Syrup:

1 cup sugar	1/2 cup butter
1/4 cup water	1 tablespoon rum extract

Generously grease and flour a 12-cup Bundt pan or tube pan; set aside. Preheat oven to 350F (175C). In a large bowl, cream butter, shortening and sugar. Add eggs one at a time, beating well after each addition. Beat in vanilla and rum extract; set aside. In a small bowl, combine sourdough starter and milk; set aside. In a medium bowl, stir together flour, baking powder, baking soda and salt. Beginning and ending with flour mixture, alternately stir sourdough mixture and flour mixture into creamed mixture. Beat well after each addition. Scrape bowl often. Pour batter into prepared pan. Bake in preheated oven 50 to 60 minutes or until a wooden pick inserted 2 inches from side comes out clean. Prepare Butter-Rum Syrup; set aside. Puncture cake 8 to 10 times with a 2-tined cooking fork. Drizzle about 1/4 of syrup over cake. Invert cake onto a plate. Remove pan. Puncture bottom of cake 8 to 10 times. Pour remaining syrup over cake. Spoon syrup from plate onto cake until completely absorbed. Cool to room temperature before cutting. Cut and serve. Makes 18 to 20 servings.

Butter-Rum Syrup:
In a small saucepan, combine all ingredients. Stir over medium heat until mixture comes to a boil.

Cakes are easily removed from baking pans that have been greased, lined with waxed paper and greased again. Remove the waxed paper immediately after turning the cake out of the pan.

Pumpkin Roll   Photo on page 142.

Topping piped through a pastry bag makes an attractive decoration.

3 large eggs
1 cup granulated sugar
2/3 cup canned pumpkin
1 teaspoon grated lemon peel
1/2 cup sourdough starter
3/4 cup plus 2 tablespoons all-purpose flour
1 teaspoon baking powder
1/4 teaspoon baking soda

1/4 teaspoon salt
2 teaspoons pumpkin pie spice
About 1/2 cup powdered sugar
Cream Cheese Filling, see below
Whipped Cream Topping, see below
1/2 cup chopped walnuts or pecans
About 12 pecan or walnut halves

Cream Cheese Filling:
2 (3-oz.) pkgs. cream cheese, softened
1/4 cup butter or margarine

1/2 teaspoon vanilla extract
1 cup powdered sugar

Whipped Cream Topping:
1/2 cup whipping cream
2 tablespoons sugar

1 teaspoon vanilla extract

Generously grease and flour a 15" x 10" baking sheet with raised edges; set aside. Preheat oven to 375F (190C). In a large bowl, beat eggs with electric mixer 5 minutes or until thick. Gradually beat in granulated sugar, pumpkin, lemon peel and sourdough starter; set aside. In a medium bowl, stir together flour, baking powder, baking soda, salt and pumpkin pie spice. Beat into sourdough mixture until blended. Pour into prepared pan. Bake in preheated oven 12 to 15 minutes or until surface springs back when touched with your fingers. Spread a cloth larger than the baking pan on a flat surface. Lightly sprinkle powdered sugar over cloth. Invert baked cake onto cloth. Remove pan. Use a sharp knife to cut 1/4 inch from all sides of cake. Discard cuttings or use for another purpose. Fold end of cloth over 1 short side of cake. Gently roll up cake and cloth. Place seam side down on a wire rack. Cool to room temperature. Prepare Cream Cheese Filling and Whipped Cream Topping. Gently unroll cooled cake. Spread filling over cake. Sprinkle with chopped nuts. Carefully roll up filled cake, removing towel as you roll. Place seam side down on a serving plate. Pipe Whipped Cream Topping in swirls along top of roll. Arrange pecan or walnut halves on top of piped topping. Refrigerate at least 30 minutes before cutting. To serve, cut in 1-inch slices. Makes about 8 servings.

Cream Cheese Filling:
In a small bowl, combine cream cheese and butter or margarine. Stir in vanilla and powdered sugar. Beat until smooth.

Whipped Cream Topping:
In a small bowl, whip cream with a rotary or electric beater until soft peaks form. Beat in sugar and vanilla. Spoon topping into a pastry bag.

Variation
Substitute mashed canned yams for canned pumpkin.

How to Make Pumpkin Roll

1/Fold ends and sides of cloth over edges of cake. Gently roll up cake and cloth.

2/When cooled, gently unroll and spread cake with prepared filling.

3/Sprinkle with chopped nuts. Carefully roll up filled cake, removing towel as you roll.

Carrot Cake

Rich and dense as a carrot cake should be.

1-1/2 cups vegetable oil
2 cups sugar
1 cup sourdough starter
2 teaspoons vanilla extract
3 eggs
2/3 cup well-drained crushed pineapple
2 cups finely-shredded carrots

3/4 cup chopped walnuts or pecans
2-1/2 cups all-purpose flour
1 teaspoon baking soda
1/2 teaspoon salt
3 teaspoons ground cinnamon
1/2 cup shredded coconut, if desired
Cream Cheese Icing, see below

Cream Cheese Icing:
2 (3-oz.) pkgs. cream cheese
3 tablespoons butter or margarine
1-1/2 to 2 cups powdered sugar

1 teaspoon vanilla extract
1 to 3 teaspoons milk, if needed

Grease a 13" x 9" baking pan; set aside. Preheat oven to 350F (175C). In a large bowl, combine oil, sugar, sourdough starter and vanilla. Add eggs one at a time, beating well after each addition. Fold in pineapple, carrots and nuts; set aside. In a medium bowl, stir together flour, baking soda, salt and cinnamon. Stir in coconut, if desired. Beat into sourdough mixture until blended. Turn into prepared pan. Bake in preheated oven 55 minutes or until surface springs back when touched with your fingers. Place pan on a rack to cool. Prepare Cream Cheese Icing. Spread icing over top of cooled cake. Cut and serve on individual plates. Makes 12 to 18 servings.

Cream Cheese Icing:
In a medium bowl, blend cream cheese and butter or margarine. Beat in powdered sugar and vanilla until smooth. If mixture is too thick to spread, stir in milk 1 teaspoon at a time.

Applesauce Cake

A prize winner!

1/2 cup shortening
1-1/2 cups sugar
2 eggs
1 cup sourdough starter
1/2 teaspoon imitation rum extract
1/2 teaspoon imitation butter flavoring
1-1/2 cups applesauce
1-3/4 cups all-purpose flour
2 teaspoons baking powder

1/2 teaspoon baking soda
1-1/2 teaspoons salt
3/4 teaspoon ground cinnamon
1/2 teaspoon ground cloves
1/2 teaspoon ground allspice
1 cup raisins
1 cup chopped walnuts or pecans
Powdered sugar for decoration

Generously grease and flour a 10-inch Bundt pan or tube pan; set aside. Preheat oven to 350F (175C). In a large bowl, cream shortening and sugar. Beat in eggs until blended. Add sourdough starter, rum extract, butter flavoring and applesauce. Beat with electric mixer on high speed 2 minutes; set aside. In a medium bowl, stir together flour, baking powder, baking soda, salt, cinnamon, cloves and allspice. Stir into sourdough mixture. Fold in raisins and nuts. Pour batter into prepared pan. Bake 1-1/4 hours or until surface springs back when touched with your fingers. Turn out of pan. Cool on a rack. Sprinkle with powdered sugar. Makes 10 to 12 servings.

Chocolate Cake

This Alaska Extension Service cake is rich, moist, very chocolate and unforgetable!

1/2 cup sourdough starter	3/4 teaspoon baking soda
1 cup water	1/2 teaspoon salt
1-1/2 cups all-purpose flour	1 teaspoon ground cinnamon
1/4 cup nonfat milk powder	1 teaspoon vanilla extract
1/2 cup shortening	2 eggs
1 cup sugar	3 (1-oz.) squares semisweet chocolate, melted
2 teaspoons baking powder	Butterscotch-Chocolate Frosting, see below

Butterscotch-Chocolate Frosting:

3 (1-oz.) squares unsweetened chocolate	1/4 teaspoon salt
1/4 cup butter or margarine	1 teaspoon vanilla extract
1/4 cup half and half or evaporated milk	About 3 cups powdered sugar
1/4 cup packed brown sugar	

In a medium bowl, combine sourdough starter, water, flour and milk powder. Set in a warm place free from drafts. Let stand 2 to 3 hours or until bubbly. Generously grease and flour two 8-inch, round baking pans or one 13'' x 9'' baking pan; set aside. Preheat oven to 350F (175C). In a large bowl, cream shortening and sugar. Beat in baking powder, baking soda, salt, cinnamon and vanilla until blended. Add eggs one at a time, beating well after each addition. Stir in melted chocolate and sourdough mixture. Beat 2 minutes with electric mixer on low speed or until blended. Pour into prepared pans or pan. Bake 40 to 45 minutes or until surface springs back when touched with your fingers. Turn out of pan or pans. Cool on a rack. Prepare Butterscotch-Chocolate Frosting. Frost cooled cake with warm frosting. Makes 8 to 10 servings.

Butterscotch-Chocolate Frosting:
In a large saucepan, combine chocolate, butter or margarine, half and half or milk, brown sugar and salt. Stir over medium heat until mixture almost comes to a boil and chocolate melts. Stir in vanilla. Gradually beat in enough powdered sugar to make a smooth spreading consistency.

Quick Chocolate Cupcakes

Chocolate lovers beware! These are so easy to make, you'll prepare them often.

1/2 cup sourdough starter	1-1/2 cups all-purpose flour
1 egg	1 cup sugar
1/2 cup milk	1/2 teaspoon baking powder
1/2 cup butter or margarine, softened	1/2 teaspoon baking soda
1 teaspoon vanilla extract	1/4 teaspoon salt
1/2 cup unsweetened cocoa powder	Goo Goo Chocolate Frosting, page 126

Grease 16 muffin cups or line with paper liners; set aside. Preheat oven to 400F (205C). In a large bowl, combine all ingredients. Do not mix until everything is in bowl. Beat with electric mixer on high speed 2 minutes. Fill prepared muffin cups 2/3 to 3/4 full with batter. Bake in preheated oven 18 to 20 minutes. Remove from muffin cups. Cool on a rack. Frost cooled cupcakes with Goo Goo Chocolate Frosting. Makes 14 to 16 cupcakes.

Pumpkin Cupcakes

A Halloween treat to delight witches and goblins.

1/2 cup shortening
1-1/2 cups sugar
2 eggs
1 cup canned pumpkin
3/4 cup milk
1/2 cup sourdough starter
2-1/2 cups all-purpose flour
2 teaspoons baking powder

1/2 teaspoon baking soda
1 teaspoon salt
2 teaspoons ground cinnamon
1/2 teaspoon ground ginger
1/2 teaspoon ground nutmeg
3/4 cup chopped walnuts or pecans
Orange-Cheese Frosting, see below

Orange-Cheese Frosting:
3 tablespoons butter or margarine
1 (3-oz.) pkg. cream cheese,
    room temperature

1/4 cup orange juice concentrate, thawed
2 to 3 cups powdered sugar

Grease 20 muffin cups or line with paper liners; set aside. Preheat oven to 350F (175C). In a large bowl, cream shortening and sugar. Beat in eggs until mixture is fluffy. Stir in pumpkin, milk and sourdough starter; set aside. In a medium bowl, stir together flour, baking powder, baking soda, salt, cinnamon, ginger and nutmeg. Beat into sourdough mixture until blended. Fold in nuts. Fill prepared muffin cups 2/3 to 3/4 full with batter. Bake in preheated oven 25 minutes. Remove from muffin cups. Cool on a rack. Prepare Orange-Cheese Frosting. Spread evenly over tops of cooled cupcakes. Makes 18 to 20 cupcakes.

Orange-Cheese Frosting:
In a medium bowl, combine butter or margarine, cream cheese and orange juice concentrate. Beat with electric mixer on high speed until mixture is light and fluffy. Gradually stir in powdered sugar, blending well after each addition, until mixture reaches spreading consistency.

tip

When recipes call for unsweetened, semisweet or sweet chocolate, use cooking chocolate, not chocolate candy.

Mocha Cupcakes

Subtle coffee flavor enhances these chocolate cupcakes.

2 (1-oz.) squares unsweetened chocolate
3/4 cup milk
1 teaspoon instant coffee powder
3/4 cup shortening
1-1/2 cups sugar
3 eggs

1/2 cup sourdough starter
2 cups all-purpose flour
1 teaspoon baking powder
1/2 teaspoon baking soda
1/2 teaspoon salt
Mocha Icing, see below

Mocha Icing:
2 cups powdered sugar
3 tablespoons unsweetened cocoa powder
2 tablespoons butter or margarine,
  softened

2 tablespoons cooled strong coffee
1 teaspoon vanilla extract
Few drops milk, if needed

Grease 24 muffin cups or line with paper liners; set aside. Preheat oven to 350F (175C). In a small saucepan, combine chocolate, milk and coffee powder. Stir over medium heat until chocolate melts. Set aside to cool 10 minutes. In a large bowl, cream shortening and sugar. Beat in eggs until mixture is fluffy. Stir in sourdough starter and cooled chocolate mixture; set aside. In a medium bowl, stir together flour, baking powder, baking soda and salt. Beat into sourdough mixture until smooth. Fill prepared muffin cups 2/3 to 3/4 full with batter. Bake in preheated oven 15 to 20 minutes or until top springs back when touched with your fingers. Remove from muffin cups. Cool on a rack. Prepare Mocha Icing. Spread over tops of cupcakes. Makes about 24 cupcakes.

Mocha Icing:
In a medium bowl, combine powdered sugar, cocoa powder, butter or margarine, coffee and vanilla. Beat until smooth. If mixture is too thick to spread, add milk 1 or 2 drops at a time.

Chocolate-Malted Cupcakes

A malted dessert that makes its own topping.

1/2 cup butter or margarine
3/4 cup sugar
2 eggs
1 teaspoon vanilla extract
1/2 cup sourdough starter
1/2 cup milk
3/4 cup instant chocolate malted-milk powder

1-1/2 cups all-purpose flour
1-1/2 teaspoons baking powder
1/4 teaspoon baking soda
1/2 teaspoon salt
1/4 cup instant chocolate malted-milk powder
1/2 cup chopped walnuts or pecans

Grease 14 muffin cups or line with paper liners; set aside. Preheat oven to 375F (190C). In a medium bowl, cream butter or margarine and sugar. Beat in eggs and vanilla until mixture is fluffy. Stir in sourdough starter and milk. In a medium bowl, stir together 3/4 cup malted-milk powder, flour, baking powder, baking soda and salt. Beat into sourdough mixture until blended. Fill prepared muffin cups 2/3 to 3/4 full with batter. Sprinkle tops evenly with 1/4 cup malted-milk powder and nuts. Bake in preheated oven 20 to 25 minutes until cupcakes pull away from side of cups. Remove from muffin cups. Cool on a rack. Makes 12 to 14 cupcakes.

Pineapple Coffeecake

Highlight your morning coffee or afternoon tea with this enticing treat.

1/3 cup sugar	1/2 cup sourdough starter
1 teaspoon ground cinnamon	2/3 cup pineapple juice, milk, water or
2 tablespoons all-purpose flour	combination
1 tablespoon butter or margarine, melted	1-2/3 cups all-purpose flour
1/3 cup well-drained crushed pineapple	2 teaspoons baking powder
1/4 cup shortening	1/4 teaspoon baking soda
1/2 cup sugar	1/2 teaspoon salt
1 egg	

In a small bowl, combine 1/3 cup sugar, cinnamon and 2 tablespoons flour. Drizzle butter or margarine over sugar mixture, then stir in with a fork. Stir in pineapple; set aside. Grease an 8-inch square baking pan; set aside. Preheat oven to 350F (175C). In a large bowl, cream shortening and 1/2 cup sugar. Beat in egg until mixture is fluffy. Stir in sourdough starter and pineapple juice, milk or water; set aside. In a medium bowl, stir together 1-2/3 cups flour, baking powder, baking soda and salt. Add to sourdough mixture. Beat until smooth. Spread in prepared pan. Spoon pineapple mixture evenly over batter. Bake in preheated oven 35 minutes or until cake pulls away from side of pan. Cool on a rack 5 minutes. Serve hot or cold. To serve, cut, remove from pan and arrange on a small platter or on dessert plates. Makes 6 to 9 servings.

Orange Cupcakes

One of these makes a nice dessert for a school lunch.

1/2 cup butter or margarine	1/2 teaspoon baking powder
3/4 cup sugar	1/2 teaspoon baking soda
2 eggs	1/4 teaspoon salt
1/2 teaspoon vanilla extract	1 cup raisins
1/2 cup sourdough starter	1/2 cup finely chopped pecans or walnuts
1 cup milk	Juice of 1 orange (6 to 8 tablespoons)
Grated peel of 1 orange (about 1 tablespoon)	1/2 cup sugar
2 cups all-purpose flour	

Generously grease and flour 14 muffin cups or line with paper liners; set aside. Preheat oven to 350F (175C). In a large bowl, cream butter or margarine and 3/4 cup sugar. Beat in eggs and vanilla until mixture is fluffy. Stir in sourdough starter, milk and orange peel; set aside. In a medium bowl, stir together flour, baking powder, baking soda and salt. Beat into sourdough mixture until blended. Fold in raisins and nuts. Fill prepared muffin cups 2/3 to 3/4 full with batter. Bake in preheated oven 20 to 30 minutes or until surface springs back when touched with your fingers. In a small saucepan, combine orange juice and 1/2 cup sugar. Stir over medium heat 3 to 5 minutes or until sugar dissolves. Remove cupcakes from muffin cups. Dip tops in orange juice mixture. Cool on a rack. Makes 12 to 14 cupcakes.

Pumpkin Roll, page 136.

Streusel-Filled Coffeecake

Buttery streusel melts into the batter as the coffeecake bakes.

Streusel, see below
1/4 cup shortening
3/4 cup sugar
1 egg
1/2 cup sourdough starter

1/2 cup milk
1-1/4 cups all-purpose flour
1-1/2 teaspoons baking powder
1/4 teaspoon baking soda
1/2 teaspoon salt

Streusel:

1/2 cup packed brown sugar
2 tablespoons all-purpose flour
2 teaspoons ground cinnamon

2 tablespoons butter or margarine, softened
1/2 cup chopped walnuts or pecans

Grease and flour an 8-inch square pan; set aside. Preheat oven to 375F (190C). Prepare Streusel; set aside. In a medium bowl, cream shortening and sugar. Beat in egg until mixture is fluffy. Stir in sourdough starter and milk; set aside. In a medium bowl, stir together flour, baking powder, baking soda and salt. Beat into sourdough mixture until smooth. Spread half of batter in prepared pan. Sprinkle with half of streusel mixture. Spoon remaining batter evenly over streusel mixture. Sprinkle remaining streusel over top. Bake 25 to 30 minutes or until cake pulls away from side of pan. Serve hot or cold. To serve, cut, remove from pan and arrange on a small platter or on dessert plates. Makes 6 to 9 servings.

Streusel:
In a small bowl, combine brown sugar, flour and cinnamon. Use a fork to stir in butter or margarine and nuts.

Chocolate Brownie Cake

Frost with Goo-Goo Chocolate Frosting, page 126.

1/2 cup butter or margarine
1 cup sugar
1 egg
1/2 teaspoon vanilla extract
1/2 cup sourdough starter
2 tablespoons milk

1 cup all-purpose flour
1/2 teaspoon baking soda
1/2 teaspoon salt
3 tablespoons unsweetened cocoa powder
1/2 cup chopped walnuts or pecans

Grease an 8- or 9-inch square baking pan; set aside. Preheat oven to 350F (175C). In a medium bowl, cream butter or margarine and sugar. Beat in egg and vanilla until mixture is fluffy. Stir in sourdough starter and milk; set aside. In a small bowl, stir together flour, baking soda, salt and cocoa powder. Stir into sourdough mixture. Stir in nuts. Pour into prepared pan. Bake in preheated oven 30 to 40 minutes or until surface springs back when touched with your fingers. Remove from pan. Cool on a rack before cutting. Makes 12 to 16 servings.

Variation

Use 1/4 cup unsweetened carob powder in place of cocoa powder; add 1/2 teaspoon ground cinnamon to flour mixture.

Pecan Coffeecake

The pecan topping is also delicious sprinkled over a fresh apple pie before baking.

Pecan Topping, see below
1/2 cup butter or margarine
1 cup sugar
3 eggs
1/2 cup sourdough starter
1/4 cup milk

2 cups all-purpose flour
2 teaspoons baking powder
1/2 teaspoon baking soda
1/2 teaspoon salt
1 cup dairy sour cream
3/4 cup raisins

Pecan Topping:
3/4 cup packed brown sugar
1 tablespoon all-purpose flour
1-1/2 teaspoons ground cinnamon

1/4 cup butter or margarine
1 cup chopped pecans

Grease a 13" x 9" baking pan; set aside. Preheat oven to 350F (175C). Prepare Pecan Topping; set aside. In a large bowl, cream butter or margarine and sugar. Beat in eggs until mixture is fluffy. Stir in sourdough starter and milk. In a medium bowl, stir together flour, baking powder, baking soda and salt. Beginning and ending with flour mixture, alternately stir flour mixture and sour cream into sourdough mixture. Beat well after each addition. Scrape bowl often. Fold in raisins. Spread mixture in prepared pan. Sprinkle with Pecan Topping. Bake in preheated oven 30 minutes or until cake pulls away from side of pan. Serve hot or cold. To serve, cut, remove from pan and arrange on a large platter or on dessert plates. Makes 12 to 18 servings.

Pecan Topping:
In a small bowl, combine brown sugar, flour and cinnamon. Cut in butter or margarine until mixture resembles fine crumbs. Stir in pecans.

Back-to-Nature Cake

Chewy with wholesome goodness.

1/2 cup shortening, butter or margarine
3/4 cup packed brown sugar
1 egg
1/2 cup sourdough starter
2 tablespoons milk
1 cup rolled oats

2 tablespoons wheat germ
2/3 cup whole-wheat flour
1 teaspoon baking powder
1/2 teaspoon salt
1/2 cup chopped walnuts or pecans
2/3 cup raisins, if desired

Grease an 8- or 9-inch square baking pan; set aside. Preheat oven to 375F (190C). In a medium bowl, cream shortening, butter or margarine and brown sugar. Beat in egg until mixture is fluffy. Stir in sourdough starter, milk, oats and wheat germ. In a small bowl, stir together flour, baking powder and salt. Stir into sourdough mixture until blended. Stir in nuts and raisins, if desired. Spoon into prepared baking pan. Bake 25 to 30 minutes or until lightly browned. Cool on a rack. To serve, cut, remove from pan and arrange on a platter or on dessert dishes. Makes about 9 servings.

Main Dishes

Sourdough cookery is so versatile you can base a whole meal on it. Meat, poultry, seafood and cheese may be combined with sourdough for a variety of taste-tempting main dishes.

Ham Crescent Rolls will be the main topic of conversation when served at a luncheon. Make and shape them ahead of time. Cover with a cloth and refrigerate them. As you attend to last-minute details, remove the rolls from the refrigerator and let them rise about one hour or until doubled in size. Bake them in a preheated 375F (190C) oven for 12 to 15 minutes. A creamed vegetable sauce or a cheese sauce makes a delicious topping.

Sourdough Pizza will please pizza fans. Make extras of these savory delights and freeze them for an evening when the whim for pizza strikes. They are easy to reheat in the microwave oven.

Frankfurters in Sourdough Buns are fun to prepare and delightful to eat. Open one end of the bun and squirt in ketchup and mustard. Make a double batch of this meal-in-a-bun. Follow the recipe directions for reheating the second batch the next day.

With one pound of ground beef, you can make wholesome Skillet Meal. It's incredibly easy and makes six good-size servings. One pound of ground beef will also make Meatball Casserole. The peppery meatballs are served over Savory Biscuits—sourdough, of course. This also makes six servings.

When you forget to thaw something for dinner, canned tuna makes Tuna Fritters that are quick and delicious.

Another fast-to-prepare main dish is Chicken à la King. It uses leftover cooked chicken. You can also use cooked turkey. Serve this famous dish over biscuits, pancakes or waffles.

Salmon Roll

Nourishing and satisfying for hearty appetites.

Salmon Filling, see below
1 teaspoon active dry yeast
2 tablespoons warm water (105F, 40C)
1 cup sourdough starter
1 teaspoon sugar

1-1/4 to 1-1/2 cups all-purpose flour
1 teaspoon baking powder
1/2 teaspoon salt
1/4 cup shortening
Cream Sauce, see below

Salmon Filling:
1/2 cup chopped celery
1/2 cup chopped green pepper
1/4 cup minced onion
3 tablespoons butter or margarine

1 (4-oz.) can chopped ripe olives
2 tablespoons chopped canned pimiento
1 (16-oz.) can salmon
1 (10-1/2-oz.) can cream-of-chicken soup

Cream Sauce:
2 to 4 tablespoons water
Reserved salmon liquid
1 tablespoon cornstarch

1/2 cup milk
Reserved cream-of-chicken soup
1 tablespoon lemon juice

Prepare and refrigerate Salmon Filling. Grease a large baking sheet; set aside. In a small bowl, sprinkle yeast over water. Set aside to soften 5 minutes. Stir in sourdough starter and sugar. In a large bowl, stir together 1-1/4 cups flour, baking powder and salt. Cut in shortening until mixture resembles coarse crumbs. Add sourdough mixture. Stir with a fork until dry ingredients are moistened. Turn out onto a lightly floured surface. Knead gently about 15 times. Add more flour if necessary. Roll out dough to a 12" x 9" rectangle. Spread Salmon Filling evenly over dough. Beginning on 1 long side, roll up jelly-roll fashion. Place roll seam side down on prepared baking sheet. Cover with a cloth and set in a warm place free from drafts. Let rise 1 hour or until about doubled in size. Preheat oven to 375F (190C). Bake Salmon Roll 30 to 35 minutes or until lightly browned. Prepare Cream Sauce. To serve, spoon Cream Sauce over Salmon Roll. Makes 6 servings.

Salmon Filling:

In a large saucepan, sauté celery, green pepper and onion in butter or margarine until vegetables are tender. Stir in olives and pimiento. Drain salmon, reserving liquid in a 1-cup measure; set liquid aside to use in Cream Sauce. Use 2 forks to flake salmon. Stir into vegetable mixture. Stir in 1/4 cup condensed soup. Reserve remaining soup and use in Cream Sauce. Refrigerate until used.

Cream Sauce:

Add water to reserved salmon liquid to make 1/2 cup. Pour into a small saucepan. Stir in cornstarch until dissolved. Stir in milk and reserved condensed soup. Stir over medium heat until mixture comes to a boil and thickens slightly. Stir in lemon juice.

Sourdough Pizza

Freeze the extra pizzas and reheat them in your microwave oven.

1 cup milk
1 teaspoon active dry yeast
2 tablespoons warm water (105F, 40C)
1-1/2 cups sourdough starter
1-1/2 teaspoons salt
2 tablespoons sugar
2 tablespoons vegetable oil or
   melted shortening

3 to 4 cups all-purpose flour
Pizza Sauce, see below
5 to 6 cups shredded mozzarella cheese or
   Monterey Jack cheese (about 1-1/2 lbs.)
1/2 lb. pepperoni sausage, thinly sliced,
   if desired

Pizza Sauce:
1 (16-oz.) can tomato sauce
1 cup chopped onion
1/4 teaspoon salt

1/4 teaspoon Italian seasoning
Pinch pepper
1/2 teaspoon leaf oregano, crushed, if desired

In a small saucepan, heat milk almost to a boil over medium heat. Do not boil. Set aside to cool 10 minutes. In a small bowl, sprinkle yeast over water. Set aside to soften 5 minutes. In a large bowl, combine sourdough starter, salt, sugar, oil or melted shortening, cooled milk and softened yeast mixture. Stir in enough flour to make a stiff dough. Turn out onto a lightly floured surface. Clean and grease bowl; set aside. Knead dough 8 to 10 minutes or until smooth and elastic. Place dough in greased bowl, turning to grease all sides. Cover with a cloth and set in warm place free from drafts. Let rise about 2 hours or until doubled in size. Prepare Pizza Sauce. Preheat oven to 425F (220C). Divide dough into 3 equal pieces for thick-crust pizzas or 4 equal pieces for thin-crust pizzas. Stretch or roll out each piece of dough to fit a 10- to 12-inch, round pizza pan. Place 1 circle of dough in each pan. Pinch edges so they stand up slightly. Spoon Pizza Sauce evenly into pans. Spread to cover dough. Top evenly with cheese. Arrange pepperoni slices evenly over cheese, if desired. Bake 20 to 25 minutes or until edge of dough browns slightly and becomes firm. Makes 3 thick-crust pizzas or 4 thin-crust pizzas.

Pizza Sauce:
In a small bowl, combine all ingredients.

tip
If you prepare and refrigerate a casserole before baking, let it stand at room temperature 15 to 20 minutes before putting it in a preheated oven. Add 10 minutes to the baking time.

Ham Crescent Rolls, page 154.

Tuna Fritters

Water-packed tuna contains about half the calories of oil-packed tuna.

1 teaspoon seasoned salt
2 cups biscuit mix
1 egg
1/2 cup sourdough starter
1/2 cup evaporated milk
2 tablespoons lemon juice
1 (12-1/2-oz.) can water-packed tuna,
   drained

2 tablespoons minced onion
2 tablespoons finely chopped green pepper
1/2 cup chopped celery
2 tablespoons freshly chopped parsley,
   if desired
Vegetable oil for deep-frying
Cheese Sauce, see below

Cheese Sauce:
1 tablespoon butter or margarine
1 tablespoon all-purpose flour
1/2 teaspoon salt

1 cup milk
2 cups shredded Cheddar cheese (8 oz.)

In a large bowl, stir seasoned salt into biscuit mix; set aside. In a medium bowl, beat egg. Stir in sourdough starter, milk and lemon juice. Stir into dry ingredients until just moistened. Stir in tuna, onion, green pepper, celery and parsley, if desired; set aside. Pour oil 3 inches deep into a deep-fryer. Heat according to manufacturer's directions. Or pour oil about 2 inches deep into a medium skillet. Heat to 375F (190C). At this temperature, a 1-inch cube of bread will turn golden brown in 40 seconds. Drop batter by teaspoonfuls into hot oil. Deep-fry 1 to 2 minutes on each side or until golden brown. Drain on paper towels. Prepare Cheese Sauce. To serve, spoon Cheese Sauce over fritters. Makes 5 servings.

Cheese Sauce:
In a medium saucepan, melt butter or margarine over low heat. Stir in flour and salt until smooth. Gradually stir in milk. Cook and stir over medium heat until slightly thickened. Stir in cheese until smooth.

Curried Shrimp Topping

Serve over Cornmeal Pancakes, page 107, or Quick Cottage Cheese Pancakes, page 101.

1/4 cup chopped celery
1/4 cup chopped green onions with tops
3 tablespoons butter or margarine
1 teaspoon curry powder or to taste
1/4 cup all-purpose flour

About 1 cup milk
1 (8-oz.) can cocktail shrimp, drained
Salt and pepper to taste
Red (cayenne) pepper to taste
1 tablespoon lemon juice

In a medium saucepan, sauté celery and onions in butter or margarine over low heat. Stir in curry powder. Stir in flour, then 1 cup milk. Cook and stir over medium heat until mixture thickens slightly. Add more milk if mixture becomes very thick. Stir in shrimp, salt and pepper to taste, red pepper to taste and lemon juice. Bring to a simmer. Serve hot over pancakes, waffles or biscuits. Makes 4 servings.

Frankfurters in Sourdough Buns

Reheat and serve this special treat while watching football games on TV.

3/4 cup hot water
3 tablespoons shortening
1/2 cup sugar
1 tablespoon salt
1 cup warm water (105F, 40C)
2 envelopes active dry yeast (2 tablespoons)

1/2 cup sourdough starter
1 egg, beaten
5 to 6 cups all-purpose flour
24 frankfurters
2 tablespoons butter or margarine, melted

In a small bowl, combine 3/4 cup hot water, shortening, sugar and salt. Stir until shortening is melted. Set aside to cool. Warm a large bowl. Pour 1 cup warm water into warmed bowl. Sprinkle yeast over warm water. Set aside to soften 5 minutes. Stir in cooled sugar mixture, sourdough starter and egg until blended. Stir in enough flour to make a soft dough. Turn out onto a lightly floured surface. Clean and grease bowl; set aside. Knead dough 8 to 10 minutes or until smooth and elastic. Add more flour if necessary. Place in greased bowl, turning to grease all sides. Cover with a cloth and set in a warm place free from drafts. Let rise 1 to 2 hours or until almost doubled in size. Grease 2 large baking sheets; set aside. Punch down dough. Turn out onto a lightly floured surface. Divide dough into 24 equal pieces. Roll or pat each piece into a 7'' x 3'' rectangle. Top each with 1 frankfurter. Wrap dough around frankfurter, covering completely. Pinch edges to seal. Arrange wrapped frankfurters on prepared baking sheets. Cover with a cloth and set in a warm place free from drafts. Let rise 45 minutes or until doubled in size. Preheat oven to 400F (205C). Bake hot dogs 20 to 25 minutes or until buns are golden brown. Remove from oven. Brush with melted butter or margarine. Serve immediately or cool on a rack. **To refrigerate or freeze:** Wrap 4 cooled buns airtight in foil or place in a container with a tight-fitting lid, making as many packages as desired. Refrigerate or freeze packaged buns. Store in refrigerator 5 days. Store in freezer about 5 months. To serve, preheat oven to 400F (205C). Bake refrigerated buns 10 to 15 minutes and frozen buns 20 to 25 minutes or until hot in center. Makes 24 servings.

Cream Sauce Vegetable Topping

Serve hot over Onion Pancakes, page 102.

3 tablespoons butter or margarine
3 tablespoons all-purpose flour
About 1 cup milk
Salt and pepper to taste

1 (10-oz.) pkg. frozen mixed vegetables, cooked, drained
1/4 cup Parmesan cheese (1 oz.)

In a medium saucepan, melt butter or margarine over low heat. Stir in flour until blended. Add milk all at once. Cook and stir over medium heat until thickened. Stir in salt and pepper to taste. Gently stir in vegetables. Spoon over biscuits, pancakes or waffles. Sprinkle with Parmesan cheese. Makes about 2 cups.

Corn Bread Chili Bake

If you've already baked Corn Bread, page 46, top it with some of the hot bean mixture.

1 lb. ground beef
1 medium onion, chopped
1/2 teaspoon salt
2 teaspoons chili powder
1/2 teaspoon garlic salt

2 teaspoons Worcestershire sauce
1 (8-oz.) can tomato sauce
1 (16-oz.) can tomatoes, chopped
1 (16-oz.) can pinto beans or kidney beans
Corn Bread Batter, see below

Corn Bread Batter:
3/4 cup cornmeal
3/4 cup all-purpose flour
2 teaspoons baking powder
1/4 teaspoon baking soda
1/2 teaspoon salt

1 egg
1/2 cup sourdough starter
3/4 cup milk
2 tablespoons vegetable oil

In a large skillet, cook and stir ground beef and onion until browned, about 10 minutes. Drain off fat. Stir in salt, chili powder, garlic salt, Worcestershire sauce, tomato sauce, tomatoes and beans. Simmer over medium heat 15 minutes. Preheat oven to 425F (220C). Lightly grease a 3-quart baking dish; set aside. Prepare Corn Bread Batter. Pour meat mixture into prepared baking dish. Spoon Corn Bread Batter evenly over meat mixture, covering completely. Bake in preheated oven 20 to 25 minutes or until bread is browned and a wooden pick inserted in center comes out clean. Makes 6 to 8 servings.

Corn Bread Batter:
In a large bowl, stir together cornmeal, flour, baking powder, baking soda and salt; set aside. In a small bowl, beat egg. Stir in sourdough starter, milk and oil. Add to cornmeal mixture. Stir until dry ingredients are just moistened.

Chicken à la King

Marvelous over Cornmeal Pancakes, page 107.

2 tablespoons chopped onion
1/4 cup minced green pepper
1/4 cup butter or margarine
1/3 cup all-purpose flour
1-1/2 cups chicken broth

1 cup evaporated milk
Salt and pepper to taste
2 cups chopped cooked chicken
2 tablespoons minced canned pimiento
2 tablespoons freshly chopped parsley

In a large saucepan, sauté onion and green pepper in butter or margarine until vegetables are tender. Stir in flour until moistened. Gradually stir in chicken broth, milk and salt and pepper to taste. Cook and stir until mixture is slightly thickened. Add chicken, pimiento and parsley. Stirring frequently, cook 5 minutes or until hot. Pour into a serving dish. Serve hot. Makes 4 to 6 servings.

Variation
Sauté 1/2 cup sliced fresh mushrooms with onion and green pepper.

Meatball Casserole

New way to top a family favorite.

1 lb. ground beef
1/4 lb. mild pork sausage
1/2 cup dry breadcrumbs
1/3 cup milk
3 tablespoons chopped onion
1 teaspoon chili powder
1/8 teaspoon pepper

1/4 cup vegetable oil
1 (10-1/2-oz.) can condensed
   cream-of-mushroom soup
1 (10-1/2-oz.) can condensed
   cream-of-celery soup
1-1/3 cups milk
Savory Biscuits, see below

Savory Biscuits:
1-1/2 cups all-purpose flour
1 tablespoon baking powder
1/4 teaspoon baking soda
1/4 teaspoon salt
1/4 teaspoon chili powder

1/3 cup shortening
1 egg
1/2 cup sourdough starter
1/4 cup evaporated milk
1-1/2 cups shredded Longhorn cheese (6 oz.)

In a large bowl, combine ground beef, sausage, breadcrumbs, 1/3 cup milk, onion, chili powder and pepper. Shape into 1-1/2-inch balls. Heat oil in a large skillet over medium heat. Brown meatballs in hot oil, adding more oil if needed. Cover and cook 15 minutes over medium-low heat. Preheat oven to 400F (205C). In a medium saucepan, combine condensed soups and 1-1/3 cups milk. Stir over medium heat until mixture begins to simmer. Arrange cooked meatballs in a 3-quart casserole dish. Pour hot soup mixture over meatballs. Set in preheated oven to keep hot. Grease a medium baking sheet; set aside. Prepare Savory Biscuits. Arrange about 8 biscuits cut side up over top of casserole. Arrange remaining biscuits on prepared baking sheet. Bake casserole 25 to 30 minutes or until biscuits are golden brown. Bake biscuits on baking sheet 15 to 20 minutes or until golden brown. Makes 4 to 6 servings.

Savory Biscuits:
In a large bowl, stir together flour, baking powder, baking soda, salt and chili powder. Use a pastry blender or fork to cut in shortening until mixture resembles coarse crumbs; set aside. In a small bowl, beat egg. Stir in sourdough starter and milk. Stir into flour mixture until dry ingredients are moistened. Turn out onto a lightly floured surface. Knead 10 to 15 times. Add more flour if needed. Dough should remain soft. Roll out or pat to an 18" x 12" rectangle. Sprinkle with cheese. Roll up from 1 long side jelly-roll fashion. Cut into 1-inch slices with a strong white thread or thin string. Place the thread or string 1 inch under end of roll with ends of thread or string extending on each side. Lift ends and cross over top of roll. Pull on thread or string until it has cut through roll. Repeat until all biscuits are cut. Makes 16 to 18 biscuits.

tip

Biscuits baked on top of a casserole remain soft on the bottom. For crisp biscuits, bake them on a baking sheet.

Ham Crescent Rolls Photo on page 149.

Glamorous way to dress up leftover ham. A meal in itself.

1/2 cup milk
2 envelopes active dry yeast (2 tablespoons)
1/2 cup warm water (105F, 40C)
1 cup sourdough starter
1/4 cup sugar
1/2 cup vegetable oil
2 teaspoons salt

4-1/2 to 5 cups all-purpose flour
Ham Filling, see below
Cream Sauce, see below
1 hard-cooked egg, sliced, for garnish
Canned pimiento strips for garnish
Paprika for garnish

Ham Filling:
1 (10-1/2-oz.) can condensed
   cream-of-mushroom soup
2 cups chopped cooked ham

2 hard-cooked eggs, chopped
1 small onion, chopped

Cream Sauce:
Reserved condensed cream-of-mushroom soup
1-1/2 cups milk
1/8 teaspoon dried leaf thyme
1/8 teaspoon dried leaf basil
2 tablespoons water

2 tablespoons cornstarch
1 (10-oz.) pkg. frozen green peas,
   cooked, drained
2 hard-cooked eggs, chopped
2 tablespoons chopped canned pimiento

In a small saucepan, heat milk almost to a boil over medium heat. Do not boil. Set aside to cool 10 minutes. Sprinkle yeast over water. Set aside to soften 5 minutes. In a large bowl, combine sourdough starter, sugar, oil, salt, cooled milk and softened yeast mixture. Gradually stir in enough flour to make a medium-stiff dough. Cover with a cloth and set in warm place free from drafts. Let rise 1 to 2 hours or until almost doubled in size. Prepare and refrigerate Ham Filling. Lightly grease 2 large baking sheets; set aside. Punch down dough. Turn out onto a lightly floured surface. Divide dough into 4 equal pieces. Shape each piece into a smooth ball, then roll out to a circle 1/4 inch thick. Cut each circle into 8 wedges. Spoon 1 rounded tablespoon Ham Filling onto outer edge of dough wedge. Roll up crescents from outside edge to point. Arrange on prepared baking sheets. Cover with a cloth and set in a warm place free from drafts. Let rise about 45 minutes or until doubled in size. Preheat oven to 375F (190C). Bake rolls 12 to 15 minutes or until golden brown. Prepare Cream Sauce. To serve, spoon Cream Sauce over hot baked crescents. Garnish with egg slices, pimiento and paprika. Makes 32 crescents.

Ham Filling:
Spoon 1/2 cup condensed cream-of-mushroom soup into a medium bowl. Stir in ham, hard-cooked eggs and onion. Reserve remaining soup for Cream Sauce.

Cream Sauce:
In a medium saucepan, combine reserved condensed cream-of-mushroom soup, milk, thyme and basil; set aside. In a small bowl, stir water into cornstarch. Stir into soup mixture. Cook and stir over medium heat until mixture comes to a boil and thickens slightly, 8 to 10 minutes. Stir in peas, eggs and pimiento.

How to Make Ham Crescent Rolls

1/Cut dough circle into 8 wedges. Spoon 1 rounded tablespoon Ham Filling onto outer edge of dough wedge.

2/Roll up triangles from outside edge to point. Arrange on prepared baking sheets. Let rise before baking.

tip

When eggs are to be stirred into a hot mixture, stir a little of the hot mixture into the eggs first, then add the egg mixture to the remaining hot mixture.

Glazed Chicken with Biscuits

The flavor of orange marmalade with the convenience of a biscuit mix make this a favorite.

2/3 cup all-purpose flour
1 teaspoon salt
1/4 teaspoon pepper
1 (3- to 3-1/2-lb.) frying chicken,
 cut in pieces

1/2 cup vegetable oil
1 cup orange marmalade
Orange Biscuits, see below

Orange Biscuits:
2-1/2 cups biscuit mix
1/4 teaspoon baking soda
1/2 cup sourdough starter

1/2 cup orange juice
2 teaspoons grated orange peel

Grease a 12" x 7-1/2" baking dish; set aside. In a pie plate, combine flour, salt and pepper. Roll chicken in flour mixture until covered; set aside. Pour oil into a large heavy skillet. Brown chicken in hot oil over medium heat, turning as needed. Cover and cook over low heat 30 minutes or until tender. Arrange chicken in prepared baking dish. Spoon 2/3 cup marmalade evenly over chicken; set aside. Preheat oven to 425F (220C). Prepare Orange Biscuits. Arrange biscuits around edge of baking dish. Press center of each biscuit with your thumb to make an indentation. Spoon about 1/2 teaspoon of remaining marmalade into each indentation. Bake in preheated oven 12 to 15 minutes or until biscuits are golden brown. Makes 6 servings.

Orange Biscuits:

In a large bowl, combine biscuit mix and baking soda. Make a well in center of dry ingredients. Add sourdough starter, orange juice and orange peel. Stir with a fork until dry ingredients are moistened. Turn out onto a lightly floured surface. Knead lightly 10 to 15 times, adding more flour if necessary. Roll out dough 1/2 inch thick. Cut biscuits with a 2-inch biscuit cutter or top of a 2-inch-wide drinking glass.

tip

Read the introductory pages in the front of this book for easy instructions on making and replenishing your starter.

Skillet Meal

Delicious as a main dish served with a vegetable and crisp garden salad or cole slaw.

1 lb. ground beef	1/2 cup sourdough starter
1 large onion, chopped	3/4 cup evaporated milk
1 cup cornmeal	1 (16-oz.) can cream-style corn
1/2 teaspoon baking powder	1/4 cup vegetable oil or shortening, melted
1-1/2 teaspoons baking soda	3 tablespoons vegetable oil or shortening
1/2 teaspoon salt	1/2 cup chopped green pepper
2 eggs	1-1/2 cups shredded Longhorn cheese (6 oz.)

In a large skillet, cook and stir ground beef and onion until browned, about 10 minutes; set aside. Preheat oven to 350F (175C). In a large bowl, stir together cornmeal, baking powder, baking soda and salt; set aside. In a medium bowl, beat eggs. Stir in sourdough starter, milk, corn and 1/4 cup vegetable oil or melted shortening. Add to cornmeal mixture. Stir until dry ingredients are just moistened; set aside. In a 10-inch iron or oven-proof skillet, heat 3 tablespoons vegetable oil or shortening over medium heat until hot. Pour in half of cornmeal batter. Spread evenly over bottom of skillet. Spoon half of meat mixture over top. Sprinkle with half of green pepper and half of shredded cheese. Repeat layers using remaining ingredients. Bake in preheated oven 45 to 55 minutes or until cornmeal mixture is no longer soft. To serve, cut into wedges. Serve hot. Makes 6 servings.

Best-Ever Granola

Serve this to your family for a best-ever breakfast, or use it in Granola Waffles, page 108.

6 cups old-fashioned rolled oats	3/4 cup vegetable oil
3/4 cup wheat germ	1/4 cup honey
1-1/2 cups shredded coconut	1/3 cup molasses
1 cup hulled raw sunflower seeds	1/2 to 1 teaspoon salt
1 (2-1/2-oz.) can sesame seeds	1 to 2 teaspoons ground cinnamon
1 to 1-1/2 cups chopped walnuts or pecans	1-1/2 teaspoons vanilla extract
3/4 cup packed dark-brown sugar	Raisins or other dried fruit, if desired
3/4 cup water	

Preheat oven to 250F (120C). In a large bowl, combine rolled oats, wheat germ, coconut, sunflower seeds, sesame seeds and nuts; set aside. In a medium saucepan, combine brown sugar, water, oil, honey, molasses, salt and cinnamon. Stir over medium heat until dissolved. Do not boil. Stir in vanilla. Pour over oat mixture. Stir until all dry ingredients are coated. Spread in two 13" x 9" baking pans or on 2 large baking sheets with raised sides. Stirring occasionally, bake in preheated oven 20 to 30 minutes. Time will depend on how thick mixture is spread and dryness desired. Cool on a rack. Stir in raisins or other dried fruit, if desired. Store in a 10- to 12-cup container with a tight-fitting lid. Store at room temperature and use within 3 to 4 weeks or freeze and use within 4 months. Makes 10 to 12 cups.

Index